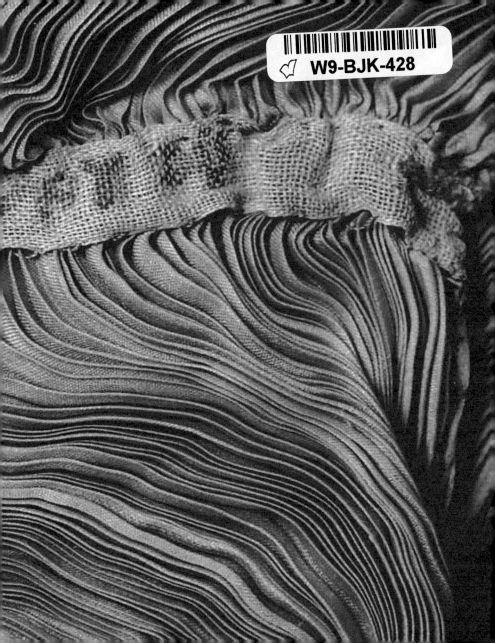

PEACOCK & VINE

PEACOCK
&
VINE

Fortuny and Morris in life and at work

A. S. BYATT

CHATTO & WINDUS
LONDON

1 3 5 7 9 10 8 6 4 2

Chatto & Windus, an imprint of Vintage,
20 Vauxhall Bridge Road,
London SW1V 2SA

Chatto & Windus is part of the Penguin Random House group of companies
whose addresses can be found at global.penguinrandomhouse.com

Penguin
Random House
UK

First published by Chatto & Windus in 2016

www.vintage-books.co.uk

A CIP catalogue record for this book is available from the British Library

HB 9781784740801
Printed and bound by C&C Offset Printing Co., Ltd., China

Design by Stephen Parker

Penguin Random House is committed to a sustainable future for our business, our readers
and our planet. This book is made from Forest Stewardship Council® certified paper.

MIX
Paper from
responsible sources
FSC
www.fsc.org   FSC® C018179

FOR GILL MARSDEN

CONTENTS

SOCIÉTÉ ANONYME

FORTVNY

DIRECTION VENISE EXPOSITION
BVREAVX PALAZZO ORFEI
805 S⁺BENETO
GIVDECCA

FORTUNY & MORRIS

We were in Venice in April and I was drunk on aquamarine light. It is an airy light, playing with the moving dark surfaces of the canals, shining on stone and marble, bringing both together in changing ways, always aquamarine. I found that an odd thing was happening to me. Every time I closed my eyes – which I increasingly did deliberately – I saw a very English green, a much more yellow green, composed of the light glittering on shaved lawns, and the dense green light in English woods, light vanishing into gnarled tree trunks, flickering on shadows on the layers of summer leaves. We were there to visit the civic museums, and I was very interested in the Palazzo Fortuny, the home of an artist of whom I had known almost nothing beyond the fact that he is the only living artist named by Proust in *À la recherche du temps perdu*. I grow more and more interested in polymaths in the arts and I have always admired those whose lives and arts are indistinguishable from each other. And as I grow older I become more and more interested in craftsmen – glass-blowers, potters, makers of textiles. My own ancestors were potters in the English pottery towns – the Five Towns in Staffordshire.

As I grow older, also, I have come to understand that my writing – fiction and thinking – starts with a moment of sudden realisation that two things I have been thinking about separately are parts of the same thought, the same work. I think, fancifully perhaps, that the excitement is the excitement of the neurones in the brain, pushing out synapses connecting the web of dendrites, two movements

becoming one. Every time I thought about Fortuny in the aquamarine clarity, I found I was also thinking about the Englishman William Morris. I was using Morris, whom I did know, to understand Fortuny. I was using Fortuny to reimagine Morris. Aquamarine, gold green. English meadows, Venetian canals. When I came back to England and started thinking about Morris, visiting the museums that were the houses where he had lived and worked, I closed my eyes and found my head full of aquamarine light, water flowing in canals, the dark of the Palazzo Pesaro Orfei.

They were both men of genius and extraordinary energy. They created their own surroundings, changed the visual world around them, studied the forms of the past and made them parts of new forms. In many ways they were opposites. Morris was an English bourgeois whose father had made an unexpected fortune in tin mining. He became a convinced and passionate socialist. Fortuny came from an aristocratic Spanish family of painters and artists and lived in an elegant aristocratic world. Fortuny's imaginative roots were Mediterranean – North Africa, Crete and Delphos. Morris was obsessed by the North and the Nordic – the Icelandic sagas, Iceland itself, the North Sea.

Mariano Fortuny was born in Granada in 1871. His father, Mariano Fortuny y Marsal, was a distinguished painter, and his mother, Cecilia de Madrazo, came also from a family of artists, architects and critics. Fortuny y Marsal died of malaria when he was only thirty-six years old – his collections of pottery, armour, textiles and carpets, as well as his paintings and etchings were an essential part of Fortuny's life and work. After his father's death his mother moved to Paris, where her brother Raimundo was a celebrated portrait painter: the family moved in a world of artists and writers. In 1889 the family moved to Venice – partly, at least, because Fortuny was allergic to horses, and suffered from asthma and hay fever. There they lived in the Palazzo Martinengo on the Grand Canal until Fortuny bought the Palazzo Pesaro Orfei in 1899. The move was partly because his mother did not approve of his companion, a French divorcee, Henriette Negrin, whom he met in Paris and who joined him in Venice in 1902, and whom he married in 1924.

Morris was born in 1834, of Welsh ancestry, in Walthamstow in a family with no aesthetic interests. He was sent to a preparatory school at the age of nine – he referred to it as a 'boy farm' – and to Marlborough College at the age of fourteen where he was desperately unhappy but stoical. He was able to do what he liked best, which was roam in the surrounding countryside. At home he developed a passion for Epping Forest, 'certainly the biggest hornbeam wood in these islands, and I suppose in the world'. He loved the hornbeams, 'magnificently grotesque' as his splendid biographer, Fiona MacCarthy, puts it, and later fought to save the forest from development. He also developed a passion for churches and for the River Thames. When he went to Oxford he became part of a group of friends, including Edward Burne-Jones, who were interested in early church architecture – they were

the Set and became the Brotherhood. The second volume of Ruskin's *The Stones of Venice*, published in 1853 was, MacCarthy says, 'an Oxford book, *the* Oxford book, of that whole period when the reading of Ruskin seemed to Morris to have been a "sort of revelation"'. In 1857 he met Jane Burden whom he married in 1859. Jane was the daughter of a stable hand, who had been discovered in a theatre by Dante Gabriel Rossetti and Burne-Jones, who collected what they called 'stunners', women of striking and unusual beauty. Morris's marriage was not happy – Janey fell in love with Rossetti, for whom she posed, and with whom she had a long affair, about which Morris, a man capable of violent rages, was generous and tolerant. When, in 1871, Morris and Rossetti took a joint tenancy of Kelmscott Manor, Morris set off for Iceland leaving Rossetti and Jane together in Kelmscott with Morris's two daughters, a gesture, MacCarthy says, which verged on the sublime.

Fortuny was happily married to Henriette, with whom he had lived for twenty-two years before the marriage. She was his partner in all his work.

I found I was musing on the two worlds, Venetian and English, seen through the images of the women who inhabited them. Morris himself was not essentially interested in painting – he cared for objects, for solid things. He made one painting of Jane in the summer and winter of 1857–8, a tall, slightly gawky woman in pink and white medieval costume, standing unsmiling beside a rumpled bed in which a small hound is sleeping. He is said to have written on it 'I cannot

paint you, but I love you'. In 1858, in a poem 'Praise of My Lady', he described her as something with the lifeless quality of ivory and metal. Her hair was 'thick and crisped wonderfully' dark and 'dead' as if forged 'Of some strange metal, thread by thread'. Rossetti started to paint her in the 1860s, over and over again, always with the same large, red, hungry, mournful mouth, distant staring eyes, and rich melancholy mass of hair. *The Blue Silk Dress* was painted in 1868 as a commission from Morris. Jane made the dress herself – Rossetti wrote to suggest that the sleeves should be 'full at the top' – and Jane's daughter May remembered it as 'a delicious, simple silk gown of shot blue and brown that was a favourite with the little girls'. In this painting Jane's nervously twisted hands display a wedding ring. In later paintings it is not there. There is something appalling, I have discovered, in looking at a whole series of Rossetti's images, more and more obsessive yet essentially all the same, brooding, dangerous, sexually greedy, too much. The best, and therefore the worst, is *Proserpine* where the brooding figure grasps the pomegranate with a bite in it, condemning her to a season in Hades. I wondered two things about this succession – are they the product of Rossetti's own disturbed imagination, or did Jane really look like that? And what effect did these images of Rossetti's feelings have on Morris, as they hung in his house or were bought by others?

Photographs of Jane Morris are remarkably like the paintings. Rossetti commissioned a series of photographic portraits of Jane, taken

in his own garden by John Robert Parsons. The face is recognisably the face of the painted woman, unsmiling, melancholy, malcontent, beautiful. Her dresses are loose, artistic. I do not have any idea at all of what she was really like. Attempts have been made, mostly by women writers, to give her a separate identity, to make as much as possible of her skilled embroidery. But she remains alien, until in old age her hair is white and her expression resigned rather than desperate.

Henry James describes meeting her in 1868.

> *Imagine a tall, lean woman in a long dress of some dead purple stuff, guiltless of hoops (or of anything else I should say) with a mass of crisp black hair heaped into great wavy projections on each of her temples, a thin pale face, a pair of strange sad, deep dark Swinburnian eyes, with great thick black oblique brows ... a long neck, without any collar, and in lieu thereof some dozen strings of outlandish beads – in fine complete. On the wall was a large, nearly full-length portrait of her by Rossetti, so strange and unreal that if you hadn't seen her you'd pronounce it a distempered vision, but in fact an extremely good likeness. After dinner ... Morris read us one of his unpublished poems, from the second series of his un-'Earthly Paradise,' and his wife, having a bad toothache, lay on the sofa, with her handkerchief to her face. There was something very quaint and remote from our actual life, it seemed to me, in the whole scene: Morris reading in his flowing antique numbers a legend of prodigies*

and terrors (the story of Bellerophon, it was), around us all the
picturesque bric-a-brac of the apartment (every article of furniture
literally a 'specimen' of something or other) and in the corner this
dark silent medieval woman with her medieval toothache.

A (to me) completely unexpected and surprising collector of Rossetti's paintings of women was the English painter L.S. Lowry, whose own world consists of dark sticklike figures moving in urban landscapes. In an interview with Mervyn Levy he said:

I don't like his women at all, but they fascinate me, like a snake.
That's why I always buy Rossetti whenever I can. His women
are really rather horrible. It's like a friend of mine who says
he hates my work, although it fascinates him.

The friend Lowry referred to was businessman Monty Bloom, to whom he also explained his obsession with Rossetti's portraits:

They are not real women ... They are dreams ... He used them for
something in his mind caused by the death of his wife. I may be quite
wrong there, but significantly they all came after the death of his wife.

The uneasiness aroused in me by the images of Morris's wife is compounded by the proliferation of cartoon drawings of Morris himself by his friends, both Burne-Jones and Rossetti. Janey is swooning and elegant: Morris is squat, fat, urgent and ridiculous. There is an exemplary caricature by Burne-Jones of 'William Morris attending his wife who lays upon a couch'. There is a drawing by Rossetti of 'Mrs Morris and the Wombat' in which Morris is a small

woolly creature (with a halo) held on a leash by proud, tormented Janey. Taken altogether these caricatures are a form of cruelty, I think, which I imagine Morris was expected to smile at and endure. He was, as I have said, known for violent rages, breaking of chairs and cutlery – but I have seen no record of his objecting to these demeaning clever

drawings. (See for instance Burne-Jones's representations of Morris at the loom, or climbing a mountain in Iceland.)

I don't think I should ever have clarified these thoughts and feelings if I had not simultaneously been trying to imagine Fortuny's domestic life in the Palazzo Pesaro Orfei.

The first image most of us see of Fortuny, frequently reproduced, is of an imposing bearded face, under a turban, over a flowing gown – a magician from the *Arabian Nights*. He lived in a world of elegant parties, extravagant theatricals, carnival and opulence. His domestic history, and his many images of his wife, are not quite what we expect. The relationship appears to have deepened slowly – they met from time to time in Paris until they decided that Henriette would join Fortuny in 1902. They arrived in Venice on the day on which the campanile of San Marco collapsed, which Fortuny's mother took as a bad omen. They lived together in the Palazzo Pesaro Orfei which Fortuny reconstructed for their workshop, studio and living space. In 1906 Arthur Evans discovered ancient fabrics during excavations in Crete – I shall come back to these – and Fortuny and Henriette decided together to make new fabrics in these old forms. She was his partner and collaborator both in the revolutionary pleated fabrics, and in the dyeing, stencilling and printing of new silk, velvet and cotton fabrics. We are told that they lived austerely and simply in their palace-workshop, with Henriette making the beds, and washing up after meals. During all their time together Fortuny made images

of Henriette, paintings, photographs, drawings – there is a wonderful charcoal drawing of a young Henriette, with a mass of dark hair, now in the Biblioteca Nacional in Madrid. She is a beautiful woman certainly, with an elegant face and hands. In the paintings particularly she has a questioning, thoughtful look, at once holding back and open. She is not voluptuous – she is what the French would describe as *bien dans sa peau*. What is striking about these repeated images – whether they were painted in 1915 or 1930 – is the feeling the painter seems to have for the model. He isn't particularly painting desire – he is painting both love and liking – this is a face he knows intimately, and cares about. There is a lovely photograph by Fortuny of Henriette in a working overall in the Palazzo Pesaro Orfei, bent over an engraved wooden block she is colouring for printing silk or velvet. And in the Museo Fortuny today there is a group of paintings hanging on a wall in the salon, a family collection, of portraits of Henriette and a self-portrait of Fortuny. Morris's domesticity was tormented, however generously he tried to accommodate his wife's needs and nerves. Fortuny seems to have created domestic calm and happiness in a glittering cavern.

THE HOUSES

I do not make pilgrimages to places where writers and painters lived. I read their work and think about their colours and words. But the museum in the Palazzo Pesaro Orfei and Morris's houses – the Red House and Kelmscott Manor, both also museums – as well as the William Morris Museum in Walthamstow, in the eighteenth-century Water House, where he lived from 1848 to 1856 – are all part of the *work* of their inhabitants, of that completeness which attracts me to both of them. Morris famously said, 'If you want a golden rule that will fit everybody this is it: have nothing in your houses that you do not know to be useful or believe to be beautiful.' This comes from a lecture on 'The Beauty of Life' where he argues, as he argues over and over again, for the making of a society where humans enjoy their work and have a sense of making beautiful and useful things. At the Kelmscott Press he printed Ruskin's 'The Nature of Gothic', a chapter of *The Stones of Venice*, with an introduction of his own in which he stresses Ruskin's belief that 'art is the expression of man's pleasure in labour; that it is possible for man to rejoice in his work, for, strange as it may seem to us today, there have been times when he did rejoice in it'. Proust seems to have slightly misunderstood Morris's beliefs – in an essay in *Pastiches et mélanges* he describes Morris as believing that a room should contain only what is useful, and that everything useful should be visible – nails for instance. But Morris, like Fortuny, was a great decorator and both men invented ingenious things, like Fortuny's lighting systems and easel, just as both made their own versions of vegetable dyes. Morris was a more and more ardent socialist as he grew older, and could never reconcile the necessary expense of the making of his beautiful furniture and fabrics with his belief that everyone should be able to live amongst beautiful and useful objects. He was also passionately opposed to the principles behind the 'restoration' of ancient buildings, and in 1878 he involved the Society for the Preservation of Ancient Buildings in a successful campaign against the restoration of the west front of St Mark's in Venice.

THE RED HOUSE

The Red House began with images of a staircase tower scribbled in a copy of Murray's *Handbook for Travellers in France* when Morris was only twenty-five, on a boat trip on the Seine. The house was designed and built for him in 1859–60 by Philip Webb, whom he had met when studying architecture in the office of the architect of the Law Courts, G. E. Street. It was in the small hamlet of Upton in Kent, in the valley of the River Cray. This very English countryside, green, unremarkable with fields, woods and a river, is reminiscent of Morris's childhood Essex. There was an orchard of apples and cherries – it is typical of Morris and Webb that they managed to plan the building around the mature trees, leaving almost all of them standing. It is simultaneously imposing and modest, secret and open. It was built in new red brick, which at the time of building would have been a startling scarlet. Pugin had already begun a fashion for using open brick rather than covering it with stucco but the Red House is different from Pugin's Gothic. It is impressive and spacious but not palatial – it has elements of old barns and farmhouses, but also a certain imposing grandeur. It has steep roofs and Gothic spires, turrets and gables, irregular windows of many sizes, round, square and rectangular, and a formidable well. Morris

looked back to the thirteenth century as an ideal age of building and craft, but the Red House is included in Nikolaus Pevsner's *Pioneers of Modern Design* as an example of the new and the strongly modern. It is part of its landscape – it had originally gardens enclosed in fences, as Georgiana Burne-Jones remembered, 'four little square gardens making a big square together, each of the smaller squares having a wattle fence round it with roses growing thickly'.

Inside, the spaces are unexpected. There is a dark hall and a twisting staircase but Morris's studio on the first floor has light on three sides from large windows, and is full of air. The German critic Muthesius described it as 'the first house to be conceived and built as a unified whole, inside and out, the very first example in the history of the modern house'. Fiona MacCarthy points out that 'the living spaces flowed from room to room, breaking down the social structures, encouraging less formal male–female relations'. The drawing room was high with exposed beams and a kind of minstrels' gallery with a door that led into the roof. The room was centred on Webb's grand, conspicuously plain red-brick fireplace with the motto ARS LONGA, VITA BREVIS. Rossetti had described Morris's early furniture as 'intensely mediaeval, like incubi and succubi'. The Red House itself he described as Topsy's Towers – a mocking reference, perhaps, to Shakespeare's 'topless towers of Ilium'.

The Red House is both an example of what drew me to Morris – the coming together of life, work and art – and also an example of an attempt to make the kind of community Morris desired – a guild of craftsmen, a fellowship of artists. Rossetti and Lizzie Siddal came there, Edward and Georgiana Burne-Jones, Swinburne the poet and Ford Madox Brown. There was a lot of play – endless games of bowls and competitions of hurling apples. Morris was the host and also the butt of what seem to be incessant japes – his waistcoat sewn up to make him appear even fatter, parcels containing nothing but packing materials, studied refusals to speak to him at the table. Burne-Jones continued to produce brilliant and cruel cartoons. But there was also artistic work – Morris and Jane painted the ceilings, the famous settle imported from the early days of Red Lion Square was decorated with images of *Dantis Amor* by Rossetti, showing the meetings of Dante and Beatrice on earth and in heaven. Morris left an unfinished painting of Paradise inside the cupboard in the hall – the characters drawn from Malory's *Morte d'Arthur* were modelled by Morris's friends, showing Sir Lancelot bringing Sir Tristram to the Joyous Garde. I find these paintings much less moving and exciting than the unexpected shapes of the house itself. There are paintings on the new plaster where the tempera didn't hold, depicting a fifteenth-century romance. They have a slightly touching amateurishness out of keeping with the strength of the red brick and the startling angles and lookouts.

Here too is the beginning of Morris's great work as a fabric designer. It is closely involved with his intelligence as a garden designer. There is an often repeated story of Jane coming home with 'some indigo-

blue dyed serge' which Morris liked for being everyday. He designed an
early version of his 'Daisy' pattern and he and Jane embroidered it on the
blue cloth. They covered the walls of the bedroom in the Red House
with the blue cloth. Morris taught Jane how to embroider. It amazes me
how many hands-on techniques of craftwork he mastered – his paintings
are stilted but his stitches are full of life, as are his papers and woven

cloths. He seems to have learned old embroidery techniques by unpicking existing work. The Morrises' two daughters, Jenny and May, were born during the years in the Red House, and May was to become a very distinguished embroidress in her own right. There are records of Morris instructing his daughters and workers in the arts – instructions which needed, May said, to be followed very exactly.

The garden and the house were one work of art – climbing plants and flowering creepers – white jasmine, honeysuckle and rose climbed the red-brick walls and edged the windows. Morris had strong beliefs about gardens. In a lecture, 'Making the Best of It', in 1879 he said:

> Large or small [the garden] should look both orderly and rich.
> It should be well fenced from the outside world. It should by no
> means imitate either the wilfulness or wildness of nature, but
> should look like a thing never to be seen except near a house.
> It should in fact look like part of a house. It follows from this
> that no private pleasure-garden should be very big, and a
> public garden should be divided and made to look like so many
> flower-closes in a meadow, or a wood, or amidst the pavement.

Morris disliked the laid-out Victorian flower beds and the works of the 'florist' who bred new flowers to increase the number and size of petals. He also disliked exotic imports – 'plants which

are curiosities only, which Nature meant to be grotesque, and which are generally the growth of hot countries where things sprout over-quick and rank'. He believed in natural materials for fences – 'when you fence anything in a garden, use a live hedge, or stones set flatwise (as they do in some parts of the Cotswold country), or timber, or wattle, or in short anything but iron'. The flowers he loved were the English countryside flowers – briar roses, violets, poppies, sunflowers, dog roses, snowdrops, single snowdrops, simple bluebells, wild honey-suckle, single sunflowers. He wrote of the sunflower:

> *the double sunflower ... is a coarse coloured and dull plant,*
> *whereas the single one ... is both interesting and beautiful, with*
> *its sharply chiselled yellow florets relieved by the quaintly*
> *patterned sad-coloured centre clogged with honey and beset with*
> *bees and butterflies.*

As this shows, he understood the flowers in many ways, and his patterns for wallpapers and woven cloths startle us into a new understanding of their forms. His first wallpaper design, done in 1864, shows single roses climbing up a trellis with busy insects and hummingbirds drawn by Philip Webb. His understanding of the relation between the repeating geometry of the regular trellis and the moving, growing geometry of the plant forms, in and out of the trellis squares made endlessly varied patterns available to him.

The work on the Red House led to the formation of a craft cooperative which, in 1861, became Morris, Marshall, Faulkner & Company, with its first workshops and offices in Red Lion Square. This became known as The Firm. They made beautiful things – furniture, stained glass, fabrics, wallpapers, painted tiles and embroidery. Morris never solved the problem of costs – the things The Firm made needed moneyed buyers as the materials were not cheap and the craftsmanship took time. Morris and Webb were at the centre – Rossetti and Burne-Jones joined in, the latter becoming a master of stained-glass design.

For two or three years they worked in Red Lion Square and travelled out to the Red House at weekends, where they were met by a covered cart specially designed by Webb. Morris hoped that the community would live there together. But in early 1862, Rossetti's wife, Lizzie Siddal, died, and two years later, when he was making plans for the Burne-Joneses to move in, Georgiana became seriously ill after the death of her premature son. Morris himself became ill and in the summer of 1865 The Firm took on a lease of larger premises in Queen Square in Bloomsbury. The Morris family moved into a flat above the Queen Square workshops. Morris could never bear to go back to the Red House, which was sold. Many of the objects were dispersed – some went to Kelmscott Manor, some to the Victoria and Albert Museum. The Red House became a private home, but now belongs to the National Trust which hopes to reassemble some of the objects and recreate the garden as far as it can. It is researching the wall hangings in the hope of restoring them too.

When I was a small child I learned Morris's poem:

> *I know a little garden-close*
> *Set thick with lily and red rose,*
> *Where I would wander if I might*
> *From dewy morn to dewy night,*
> *And have one with me wandering.*
>
> *And though within it no birds sing,*
> *And though no pillared house is there,*
> *And though the apple-boughs are bare*
> *Of fruit and blossom, would to God*
> *Her feet upon the green grass trod,*
> *And I beheld them as before ...*

As long as I had known about the Red House I had a mental image of the house, the garden, and the countryside with fields, hedges and river. We went there to visit, only to find that the solid edges of urban London have surrounded and almost swallowed it. The enclosed garden is defensive in a way it was not when it was made. It is outside its time, and very moving.

KELMSCOTT MANOR

In June 1871 Morris and Rossetti took Kelmscott Manor near Lechlade in Gloucestershire on a joint lease. Morris wrote to his friend Charley Faulkner:

> *whither do you guess my eye is turned now? Kelmscott, a little*
> *village about two miles above Radcott Bridge – a heaven on earth;*
> *an old stone Elizabethan house like Water Eaton, and such a*
> *garden! close down on the river, a boat house and all things handy.*

Morris loved the house because of its simplicity – he described it as 'a beautiful and strangely naïf house' and wrote of it as:

> *a house that I love; with a reasonable love I think ... so much has the*
> *old house grown out of the soil and the lives of those that lived on it:*
> *needing no grand office architect ... but some thin thread of*
> *tradition, a half-anxious sense of the delight of meadow and acre*
> *and wood and river ... a liking for making materials serve one's turn.*

He wrote also:

The land is a little land ... all is measured, mingled, varied, gliding easily one thing into another: little rivers, little plains, swelling speedily changing uplands, all beset with handsome orderly trees ... all is little; yet not foolish and blank, but serious rather, and abundant of meaning for such as choose to seek it: it is neither prison nor palace but a decent home.

Morris loved the gabled grey-stone building, made, Fiona MacCarthy tells us, from the coarse local oolite stone of the Thames Valley – he loved 'the entrances and exits, surprise views, odd heights and depths and juggling with spaces'. 'What gave him great delight was the way in which the slates had been "sized down" by the roofers, so that they used the small ones at the top, graduating to larger ones down towards the eaves. The "ordered beauty" of the Kelmscott roofs reminded him of birds' feathers, fishes' scales.'

Morris had said he was looking for a 'house for the wife and kids ... a little house deep in the country where she and the children are to spend some months each year'. But, as later writers have pointed out, he was perhaps also trying to find somewhere where the relations between Rossetti and Janey would be less visible. What in fact happened was that Rossetti settled into Kelmscott Manor and Morris – after his first trip to Iceland in the summer of 1871 – felt himself unable to go there. It was clearly unbelievably painful. By September 1872 Rossetti was talking about settling permanently in Kelmscott. Morris finally

admitted in an unusual outburst in a letter:

> *another quite selfish business is that Rossetti has set himself down at Kelmscott as if he never meant to go away; and not only does that keep me away from that harbour of refuge (because it is really a farce our meeting when we can help it) but also he has all sorts of ways so unsympathetic with the sweet simple old place, that I feel his presence there as a kind of slur on it: this very unreasonable though when one thinks why one took the place, and how this year it has really answered that purpose: nor do I think I should feel like this about it if he had not been so unromantically discontented with it and the whole thing which made me very angry and disappointed.*

Rossetti in his early days at Kelmscott wrote of his pleasure in long walks with Mrs Morris, whom he painted in *The Water Willow* in 1871, holding branches of willow beside the water, with the River Thames and the gables of Kelmscott in the background. He invited friends and models to visit, and also painted, obsessively, several versions of Jane as Proserpine – with clinging ivy. He painted a total of fifty-seven studies of her, the best done at Kelmscott. But he was addicted to chloral and whisky, and did not like being left in Kelmscott when Jane and the children were with Morris. In June 1872 he had a breakdown and in 1874, after Morris had reorganised his business, cutting Rossetti out of the company, he abruptly left.

Morris was able to return to his house, his favourite retreat from work in Queen Square.

Life in Kelmscott Manor was austere – there were three adjacent outdoor privies, that can still be seen, and no running water. Guests such as George Bernard Shaw found the water frozen in the glass by their bedside. Charles M. Gere made the iconic woodcut of Kelmscott Manor which was used in Morris's *News from Nowhere* – an image of the main front of the manor with the path, flanked by standard roses, leading up to the entrance door, plants growing up the stone walls and a flock of birds in the sky. He recalled staying at Kelmscott Manor 'in a small room adjoining Morris's study, where he could be heard writing with quill pens which he threw down as they blunted'. He wrote:

> *At Kelmscott manor I stayed in a little powder closet which opens from the Tapestry Room. [This contained some original tapestries of the tale of Samson and Delilah, dating from 1600.] Morris used to bring me in a can of hot water in the morning. He used to tumble out of bed, have his tub, slip into his blue shirt and blue suit, thrust a brush – or maybe only his hands – through his curly hair and beard – all the work of a few moments – and he was ready for the day's adventure.*

Morris liked everything solid and large; the washbasins and jugs were of massive proportions in earthenware; his teacup and porridge bowl the same. He liked his bread in solid chunks; on one occasion

Gere cut some bread at breakfast far too thin for his taste. A moment later he arrived and with a shout of disgust roared out, 'Who cut this bread?' Walks with Morris around the country were always a treat and an education. It was on one of these walks that he said, 'You must enjoy a work of art in your stomach.'

Morris loved the River Thames, and all through his life lived or worked close to it. May Morris, his daughter, in her biography of her father, recalls him talking to her about the willows on the banks, and teaching her to see their structures. 'He noted every turn of a leaf or attachment of a stem, watched every bird on the wing with keen alert eye: nothing in the open air escaped him.'

He was interested in structure, not symbolism. Rossetti's *Water Willow* perhaps shows the usual sadness of 'weeping willow'. Morris's wallpaper, Willow, is a masterpiece of observation, both of geometry and of the real shapes and forms of growing plants. As May said, 'Without being a "symbol" of any special thought, each of the more important patterns for papers or chintz had its mark, its standing or its bit of story'. Morris's chintzes of the mid-1870s – such as Honeysuckle, Iris and Marigold – were made after hours of sketching and study. He was already learning to make vegetable dyes from roots, flowers and the willow twigs themselves – another passion he shared with Fortuny.

And he listened to all the birds. Birds on roofs, birds in trees, birds in and on water. In the late summer of 1871 he wrote:

*The birds were very delightful about us; I have been of late so
steeped in London that it was quite a fresh pleasure to see the rooks
about, who have been very busy this showery weather. There was
no lack of herons in these upper waters, and in the twilight the stint
or summer snipe was crying about us and flitting from under the
bank and across the stream: such a clean-made, neat-feathered,
light grey little chap he is, with a wild musical little note like all
the moor-haunting birds.*

We are told that he mentions herons 'stalking about the fields in the
gravest manner'; a kingfisher taking a fish, and a 'sailing' owl.[*]

Kelmscott Manor makes a strange and mysterious appearance
at the end of Morris's pastoral vision of the future, *News from Nowhere
(Or an Epoch of Rest)* published in 1890. In this tale the central character,
William Guest, having gone to bed in winter after a meeting of the
Socialist League wakes up in summer and finds himself in the future,
in a socialist society without private property, money, cities, class
system. It is an agrarian society where people work because work is
pleasurable, and make things that are naturally beautiful for their
homes. Children do not go to school but find things out naturally
through play and exploration. At the centre of the story is a boat
journey up the Thames from the (clean) London shore into the

[*] I am much indebted to *The Gardens of William Morris*, by Jill, Duchess of Hamilton,
Penny Hart and John Simmons. This quotation is on page 63.

countryside Morris loved. The story is full of conversation and objects, but at the end, with Ellen, whom he loves and loses, he visits what she describes as 'this many-gabled old house built by the simple country-folk of the long-past times, regardless of all the turmoil that was going on in cities and courts, [which] is lovely still amidst all the beauty which these latter days have created; and I do not wonder at our friends tending it carefully and making much of it.'

Kelmscott in *News from Nowhere* is a presence both ghostly and empty and enduring.

> *We went in and found no soul in any room as we wandered from room to room, – from the rose-covered porch to the strange and quaint garrets among the great timbers of the roof, where of old time the tillers and herdsmen of the manor slept, but which a-nights seemed now, by the small size of the beds, and the litter of useless and disregarded matters – bunches of dying flowers, feathers of birds, shells of starlings' eggs, caddis worms in mugs, and the like – seemed for the time to be inhabited by children.*

> *Everywhere there was but little furniture, and that only the most necessary and of the simplest forms. The extravagant love of ornament which I had noted in these people elsewhere seemed here to have given place to the feeling that the house itself and its associations was the ornament of the country life amidst which it*

had been left stranded from the old times, and that to re-ornament
it would but take away its use as a piece of natural beauty. We sat
down at last in a room over the wall which Ellen had caressed, and
which was still hung with old tapestry, originally of no artistic
value, but now faded into pleasant grey tones which harmonized
thoroughly well with the quiet of the place, and which would ill have
been supplanted by brighter and more striking decoration.

Morris's daughter May became a highly accomplished artist and embroidress. Morris died in 1896, and in 1923, at the age of sixty-two, May gave up her London home and came to live permanently in Kelmscott. She was torn between her desire for the house to continue to feel 'lived-in' and for it to remain unchanged from the house Morris had known and loved. It is now in the process of being restored, as a museum, to something more like Morris's home than it became after various alterations and occupations. William Morris's great bed can be seen there in all its glory, with the pelmet and bedspread beautifully embroidered by May. Round the pelmet runs his 'Inscription for an Old Bed'.

The wind's on the wold
And the night is a-cold,
And Thames runs chill
'Twixt mead and hill;

But kind and dear
Is the old house here,
And my heart is warm
Midst winter's harm.
Rest, then, and rest,
And think of the best
'Twixt summer and spring,
When all birds sing
In the town of the tree,
And ye lie in me
And scarce dare move,
Lest the earth and its love
Should fade away
Ere the full of the day.
I am old and have seen
Many things that have been –
Both grief and peace
And wane and increase.
No tale I tell
Of ill or well,
But this I say,
Night treadeth on day.
And for worst or best
Right good is rest.

PALAZZO PESARO ORFEI

We went to the Museo Fortuny, in the Palazzo Pesaro Orfei, on a sunny spring day. Fortuny bought the house at the end of the nineteenth century – he was already working there in 1899 – and moved into it with Henriette in 1902. It was built from the mid-fifteenth century, and stands, not on the waterfront of a canal, but between the Campo and the Rio di Ca' Michiel. Ruskin admired it for its 'masculine' elegance, and it has two intricate facades on the Campo and the Rio, with rows of large mullioned windows – with round 'bottle-bottom' panes, and interior courtyards and loggias, where a wisteria grows strongly. It took its full name Palazzo Pesaro degli Orfei from an eighteenth-century musical society known as the Accademia d'Orfeo which had been a tenant. It was later occupied by another philharmonic company, the Società Apollinea who later moved to the newly opened Teatro La Fenice. When Fortuny first saw it, it had fallen away from its rich days when it had housed important collections of paintings, and had been divided into rented apartments for workers. When Fortuny moved into his first two rooms there were 350 craftsmen and others working there. Fortuny acquired more and more space, bit by bit, and was finally able to restore the original Venetian spaces inside the building. These consisted of two large *porteghi* – on the ground floor and on the

first floor – and above them huge attic spaces. A *portego* is a long salon with small rooms at each end where work is done. The first-floor *portego* was where the Fortunys lived and worked. The second floor was the workshop where over a hundred workers made the silk and velvet fabrics, and stitched the wonderful clothes. When we went in for the first time I was dazzled by the darkness – the walls are dark, the rooms are dark, and inside them Fortuny's paintings and fabrics glimmer and glitter on the walls. When I went to Topkapi in Istanbul I remember my guides explaining that this was the richness of an originally nomadic culture – cherishing carpets and hangings and things which could be moved, redeployed, folded. Fortuny's spaces seem to have something of this quality, Arabic or oriental. I was pleased to read that one winter, to protect himself and his work from the cold, he did in fact put up a giant marquee in the *portego*.

Fortuny's interest in textiles was first aroused by his mother's rich collection of ancient fabrics in a trunk, which she would open to show her guests amazing dyes, designs and weaving. Henri de Régnier described her collection in his book *L'Altana, ou la vie Vénitienne*.

> She made her first purchase in Spain: a blood-red piece of old velvet, embellished with pomegranates ... Mother and daughter open a massive chest in the corner of the room. Here, lightly folded, lie hundreds of fabrics, which they slowly and carefully draw out to show me. The first appears: a fine piece of dark blue velvet made in

the fifteenth century, goffered with stylish arabesques. The shade is strange, deep and pure, like the colour of night. Slowly, slowly, the magic is wrought: one by one, the fabrics are brought forth, unfolded, viewed, and cast over the back of an armchair or a sofa later to be replaced in the great cassone where they reside.

Looking at the *portego* in the Palazzo Fortuny, one can see the continuing influence of this changing richness – it is both a showroom, and a living space, with works of art and craft, sometimes with mannequins with Fortuny garments draped around them, sometimes with screens or settles over which wonderful fabrics are apparently casually thrown. I am particularly intrigued by a painting by Fortuny himself of the first-floor salon. It is almost like a theatre set with two ceiling-high dark curtains dividing the room, open to show the riches beyond. Figures in armour glimmer dimly – one oriental, one European? – inside the curtains. In the inner part a pale statue stands over draped cloths, with another dark armed figure just visible in front of her. Some kind of drapery or flag is suspended from the ceiling – red and cream with a red-and-blue edge. The ceiling is high and dark with red-lit beams. A flag hangs from this and disappears behind the curtain. There are paintings on the walls but we see only the glimmer of gold frames. There is one frame leaning casually against a wall. There is a pale pillar. And a piece of furniture with a startling turquoise pattern, also in shadow. Everything is rich and provisional. There is a kind of

almost-clothes-horse with layers of garments thrown over a red-gold drape. In the foreground is a clutter of tools of the trade – a litter of paper, in a roll, and folders, sketches, a ruler. On the left edge – so that it is the thing I at least noticed last – is a painting, almost white and black, small and discreet, of the painter painting, less real than the richness of the orderly clutter. He is making and altering a world.

To think about Fortuny is to think about light. Light reflected from silk and velvet – and flesh – light on water and stone, airy light, dense light, almost infinitely varied coloured light. In the book on Fortuny by Anne-Marie Deschodt and Doretta Davanzo Poli, there are two plates showing women wearing Fortuny silk-velvet capes, seen from behind and looking out over the water. The first is seen at dusk, with the Palladian church of San Giorgio Maggiore across the water. Deschodt writes: 'The short silk-velvet cape catches the breeze of the sirocco. It is printed in silver and gold with Coptic designs at the shoulders, Persian tree-of-life palmettes, and cuffs and border motifs inspired by Hellenistic Greek ornamentation'. The coat is an inky brown-black colour, the formal yet lifelike trees shine soft silver, the water and the sky are an inky dark blue, one expanse with a hint of rosy light in the indigo. Both garment and sky, both water and shadowy building, are unworldly and strange. In the other photograph the woman is standing in the mouth of an alleyway wearing, Deschodt says, 'a long velvet cape printed with a gold leaf pattern inspired by Chinese and Japanese textiles. Its warm tones harmonize perfectly with the pink-and-beige brickwork of a Venetian alleyway. In the distance across the water lies the island of the Giudecca, with the Palladian church of the Redentore'. Here the spread of fabric covered with shining and shadowy gold and silver leaves glints in the darkness. The water, seen again in front of the woman's head, is a pale blue, with silver waves; the paving stones in the sun are a pale pink ochre, the church is a graceful shadow in muted white stone and pink tiles. The sun is soft on the pale sky and water. Again it is both real and unreal, in this world and unworldly.

In *À la recherche du temps perdu*, Proust's narrator describes the Fortuny dress, 'bleu et or doublée de rose', which Albertine prefers to all the other dresses she is given. Gérard Macé has written a wonderful book, *Le manteau de Fortuny*, in which he describes the significance for Proust of the work of Fortuny. He quotes Proust's description of the dress and says 'la robe de Fortuny n'est que l'ombre de Venise, et comme le manteau un peu plus tard, une métaphore filée autant qu'une étoffe'. (Fortuny's gown is no more than the shadow of Venise, and, like the cloak a little later, a woven metaphor as much as a fabric.) He quotes Proust's description at length.

> *Elle était envahie d'ornementation arabe comme Venise, comme*
> *les palais de Venise dissimulés à la façon des sultanes derrière un*
> *voile ajouré de pierres, comme les reliures de la Bibliothèque*
> *Ambrosienne, comme les colonnes desquelles les oiseaux orientaux*

qui signifient alternativement la mort et la vie, se répétaient dans le miroitement de l'étoffe, d'un bleu profound qui au fur et à mesure que mon regard s'y avançait se changeait en or malléable par ces mêmes transmutations qui, devant la gondole qui s'avance, changent en métal flamboyant l'azur du grand canal. Et les manches étaient doublées d'un rose cerise, qui est si particulièrement vénitien qu'on l'appelle rose Tiepolo.

It swarmed with Arabic ornaments, like Venice, like the Venetian palaces hidden like the sultan's wives behind a screen of pierced stone, like the bindings in the Ambrosian Library, like the columns from which the oriental birds that symbolised alternately life and death were repeated in the mirror of the fabric, of an intense blue which, as my gaze extended over it, was changed into a malleable gold, by those same transmutations which, before the advancing gondola, change into flaming metal the azure of the Grand Canal. And the sleeves were lined with a cherry pink, which is so peculiarly Venetian that it is called Tiepolo pink.

When Albertine flees the narrator she takes away only one of his presents – a Fortuny cloak in sombre dark blue. In *Les Oeuvres d'art imaginaires chez Proust*, Michel Butor distinguishes between '*le roman robe*' and '*le roman cathédrale*' – two different metaphors for the work itself. Seeing Fortuny garments beside Venetian churches gives a new

depth and force to these alternative metaphors.

Fortuny worked with light itself. All his life he took photographs of all sorts of things and people – he was an early user of the wide-angle lens to show the Grand Canal, and the Piazzetta San Marco, but he studied the shadows in the alleys of Venice. He photographed women, naked and clothed – his images are about light and substance rather than provocation, I think. He seems to have been a man who liked women, who was interested in them. He photographed Henriette

in many lights and from many angles, but always with understanding, affection, endless interest. He photographed the interiors of the Palazzo Pesaro Orfei, the shelves in his library, with the rows of volumes he had covered himself. He photographed the lights he had designed. He took out a patent for a new kind of photographic paper, and was among the earliest to use the Lumière brothers' new coloured films.

Fortuny invented large numbers of lights, including the famous 'Saracen shield', a circular silk ceiling lamp, and various dangling silk lamps in the form of reticules or long purses. He made spiral *cesendelli* in glass and in silk. He made 'firefly' table lamps. But he also used electricity to make many different very modern reading and table lamps, and the image of these introduces the aspect of the interior of the Palazzo Pesaro Orfei I have not yet mentioned – it is full of invented machines, including electric lamps of different heights and with different stands to hold brushes or other implements. There are many different easels often with wheels and with the seat and the easel as parts of the same travelling equipment. The library contains two large presses, one old, one already electric. There are arrangements of small tools – drill bits for instance. Fortuny designed his own reading desk and curved shelving. There are cupboards full of pigments. The crafts and their tools are an essential part of the brilliant spaces – I was reminded of William Morris, having learned to weave, buying a loom and setting it up in his bedroom. During his lifetime, according to Anne-Marie Deschodt, Fortuny took out more than fifty patents in Paris.

> *Among the most notable are a system for indirect theatrical lighting; an arc lamp that can function in any position; a dimmer switch or rheostat for variable lighting; a curved, collapsible theatrical backdrop or cyclorama called the Fortuny dome; a method of pleating fabric in 'wavy pleats'; a method of polychrome printing on textiles; a transparent curtain for vitrines or bookcases; a system of propulsion for ships that allows them to swim in the water like eels;*

*and a hat stand of superior ability (the ordinary sort being liable to
fall over), with a broad conical base set in a heavy socle, and a
spring lodged in the centre to connect the stand with the base.*

One of his most important inventions was indeed the new form of
stage lighting which enabled him to contribute in an extraordinary way
to Wagner's *Gesamtkunstwerk* (total work combining all art forms). In 1901
he patented the technique of indirect – reflected – lighting for the stage.
In 1904 he describes looking at a sheet of white paper in a dark studio:

*If one lets a ray of sunlight into a darkened room, one will see a shaft
of light piercing the air, but the room will not be lit up. If one then
introduces a white leaf of paper in front of this shaft, the light will
break up and illuminate the whole room; and yet the actual quantity
of light entering still remains the same in both cases. This experiment
proves that it is not the quantity but the quality of light that makes
things visible and allows the pupil of the eye to open properly.*

He invented, and refined, a system of reflected electric light for
the stage – a dome, white at first and then with mixed and reflected
colours. Wagner's operas, in the days of gas lighting, had had endless
painted backdrops. Fortuny was now able both to compose the
setting onstage, conducting light as one conducts music, and to do
away with the empty spaces between elements of the painted sets.

He began with a white cement dome, but moved on to a collapsible light one. He was the inventor of the gallery behind the audience where the lighting artist sits.

> To sum up, my system is composed of three parts: a system of lighting by means of reflection; a system of stage decoration by means of reflection, allowing for the use of a concave surface to make skies and distant views; last, and most important, a complete reform of the visual element in the theatre, because it can be said

for the first time that theatrical scenery will be able to transform itself in tune with music, with the latter's domain, that is to say in 'time' whereas hitherto it has only been able to develop in 'space'. This last ability is of supreme importance for the staging of the works of Richard Wagner.*

Morris too was both craftsman and inventor. Under 'craft skills' in the index to Fiona MacCarthy's biography appear 'brass rubbing; calligraphy; cooking; clay modelling; dyeing; illuminated mss; painting and drawing; paper making; stone carving; tapestry; textiles, woven; wood carving; wood engraving'.

Like Fortuny, he collected and perfected his own tools for these pursuits. MacCarthy tells one particularly attractive story of him at work in 1870 rediscovering the ancient technique of gilding. It is worth quoting in full.

The gilding of the letters and the ornament of illuminated manuscripts is a complex, and chancy, craft in itself: a gesso base is laid and the gold-leaf attached and burnished. Traditionally the gesso was prepared from an arcane mixture of slaked plaster of Paris, white lead, bole and such adhesives as sugar, glue and egg. The raised gold was technically very problematic. May remembered sheets of paper strewn about her father's study for years afterwards covered with

* Guillermo de Osma, pp. 66 and 70.

Of the valiant Knights in France and England

Liege, affermyng thus howe that many noble persons haue oft tymes spoke of the
warres of Fraunce & of Inglande, & perad-
uenture knewe nat lustely the trouth ther-
ofe, nor the true occasyons of the fyrst
mouyngis of suche warres, nor how the
warre at length contynued: but now I trust
ye shall here reported the true foundation
of the cause; & to thentent that I wyll not
forget, mynyoahe, or abrydge the hystory
in any thyng for defaute of langage; but
rather I wyll multiply & encrease it as ner
as I can, folowynge the trouth from poynt
to poynt in apekyng and shewyng all auentures sith the natiuite of the noble kyng
Edward the III. who reigned kyng of England, & achyued many perilous auentures,
and dyuers great batelles addressed, and
other featis of armes of great prowes, syth
the yere of our Lorde God MCCCxxvj. that
this noble kyng was crowned in Ingland.

FOR generally suche as were with
hym in his batels and happy fortunate auentures, with his peple in
his absence, ought ryght well to be takyn
and reputed for valiant and worthy of renowne; and though there were great plenty
of sondrye parsonages that ought to be
prayased and reputed as souereignes, yet
among other and principally ought to be
renowned the noble propre persone of the
forsaid gentyll kyng; also the prynce of
Walys his son, the duke of Lancaster, syr
Reignolde lorde Cobham, syr Gualtier of
Manny of Heynaulte, knyght, syr Johan
Chandos, syr Fulque of Harley, and dyuers other, of whom is made mencion hereafter in this present boke, bicause of theyr
valyant prowes; for in all batels that they
were in, most commonly they had euer the
renowne, both by land and by se, accord-
yng to the trouth. They in all theyr dedis
were so valyant that they ought to be reputed as souereignes in all chyualry; yet
for all that, suche other as were in theyr
company ought nat to be of the lesse value, or lesse sette by.

ALSO in Fraunce, in that tyme, there
were founde many good knyghtis,
stronge and well expert in featis of
armes: for the realme of Fraunce was nat
so disconfited but that alwayes ther were
people sufficient to fyght withal; and the
kyng Philyppe of Valoys was a right hardy and a valiaunt knyght; and also kyng
Johan, his sonne; Charles, the kyng of
Behaigne, the erle of Alanson, the erle of
foyz, syr Saintre, syr Arnold d'Andre-
hen, syr Boucicault, syr Guichard d'Angle,
the lordes of Beaujeu, the father and the
sonne, and dyuerse other, the whiche I can
nat theyr names, of whom hereafter ryght
well shall be made mencion in tyme & place
conuenient to say the trouth, and to mayn-
teigne the same: all such as it in cruel batels
haue ben seen abydyng to the disconfecture,
sufficiently doyng theyr deuoyr, may wel be
reputed for valyant and hardy, what soeuer
was theyr aduenture.

Here the mater speketh of some of the
predecessours of Kyng Edwarde of Ingland. Capitulo III.

FIRST, the better to
entre into the mater
of this honorable and
pleasaunt hystory of
the noble Edwarde,
kyng of Inglande, who
was crowned at Lon-
don the year of our
Lorde God MCCC-
xxvj. on Christmas-
day, lyuyng the kyng his father and the
quene his mother. It is certayne that the
opynyon of Inglisshemen moost comonly
was as than, and often tymes it was seen
in Ingland after the tyme of kyng Arthure,
how that betwene two valyant kynges of
Ingland, ther was moost comonly one bi-
twene them of lesse sufficiancy, both of
wytte and of prowes; and this was ryght
well aparant by the same kyng Edward the
thyrde; for his graundfather, called the
good kyng Edward the fyrste, was ryght
valyant, sage, wyse, & hardy, auenturous
and fortunate in all featis of warre, and had
moche ado agaynst the Scottis, and con-
quered them thre or foure tymes; for the
Scottes coude neuer haue victory nor in-
dure agaynst hym.

AND after his disseace his sonne of
his first wife, who was father to the
said good kyng Edward the thyrd,
was crowned kyng, & called Edward the II.
who resembled nothyng to his father in
wyt nor in prowes, for all may not be aourn-
ed of good vertues, but gouerned and kept
his realme ryght wyldly, & ruled hymselfe
by oynyster counsell of certayne parsons,
whereby at length he had no profytte nor
lande, and fell into the hate and indygna-
cion of his people, as ye shall here after;
but they shewed hym not of his secret fol-
lies ere he had wrought many great euyls
and cruell iustyces on the noble men of his
realme. Englysshemen bear nat for a
while, but in the end they paye so cruelly as
the lilie can not be shewn therof. And a lord
lyeth down & ryseth up in much great pa-
ryl of those whom they gouern, for they
loue hym not nor honour hym if he be not
victoryous, and loueth nat armes and war-
ryng on his neighbours, and in especyall
theym that be mightier and of more wealth
then he, and they have this condycion and
hold thys opynyon, and haue euer held it,

HERE BEGYNNETH THE PROLOGE OF SYR JOHAN FROISSART OF THE CHRONICLES OF FRAUNCE, INGLANDE, AND OTHER PLACES ADJOYNYNGE

The First Chaptre.

THAT the honorable and noble aventures of featis of armes, done & achyued by the warres of Fraunce and Inglande, shulde notably be inregistered, and put in perpetuall memory, wherby the prewe & hardy may haue ensample to incourage them in theyr well doyng, I, syr Johan Froissart, wyll treat and recorde an hystory of great louage and preyse: but, or I begyn, I require the sauyour of all the worlde, who of nothyng created al thynges, that he wyll gyue me suche grace and vnderstandyng, that I may continue and perseuer in such wyse, that who so this proces redeth orhereth, may take pastaunce, pleasure, and ensaumple It is said of trouth, that al buyldynges are masoned & wroughte of dyuerse stones, and all great ryuers are gurged and assemblede of diuers surges and sprynges of water: in lyke wyse all sciences are extraught & compiled of diuerse clerkes, of that one wryteth, another paraurenture is ignorant; but by the famous knowen in one place or other.

WHAN to attaygne to the mater that I haue entreprised, I wyll begyn, fyrst, by the grace of God and the blessed Virgyn our Lady Saynt Mary, from whom all comfort and consolation procedeth, and wyll take my foundation out of the true cronicles somtyme compyled by the right reuerend, discrete and sage maister Johan la Bele, somtyme chanon in Saint Lambartis of Liege, who with good herte & due diligence dyd his true deuoure in wrytyng this noble cronicle, and dyd contynue it all his lyfes days, in folowyng the trouth as nere as he myght, to his great charge and coste in achyng to procure and to haue the parfight knowlege thereof. He was also in his lyfes days welbeloued, and of the secret counsayle with the lorde sir Johan of Haynaulte, who is often remembred, as reason requyreth, here after in this boke; for of many fayre & noble auentures he was chiefe causer, & to the kyng right nigh, & by whose meanes the said syr Johan la Bele myght well knowe and here of many dyuers noble dedes. The whiche here after shal be declared.

TROUTH is it, that I who haue entreprised this boke to ordeyne for pleasure and pastaunce, to the whiche alwayes I have been inclyned, & for that intent I haue folowed and frequented the company of dyuerse noble & great lordes, as well in Fraunce, Inglande, and Scotlande, as in diuerse other countries, and haue had knowlege by them, and alwayes to my power iustly haue inquired for the trouth of the dedis of warre and auentures that haue fallen, and specially syth the great batell of Poytyers, where as the noble kynge Johan of France was takyn prisoner, as before that tyme I was but of a yonge age or vnderstandyng. Howe be it I toke it on me as soone as I come from scole, to wryte and recite the sayd boke, & bare the same compyled into Ingland, and presented the volume thereof to my Lady Phelyppe of Heynaulte, noble quene of Inglande, who right amyably receyued it to my great profite & auancement.

AND it may be so, that the same boke is nat as yet examyned nor corrected so iustely as suche a case requyreth: for featis of armes derely bought & achyued, the honor therof ought to be gyuen & truly deuided to them that by prowes & hard trauayle haue deserued it Therfore to acquyre me in that bihalfe, & in folowyng the trouth as near as I can, I Johan Froissart haue entreprysed this hystory on the foresaid ordynaunce & true fundacion, at the instaunce and request of a dere lorde of myn, Robert of Namure, knight, lorde of Bewfort, to whom entierly I owe loue and obeysaunce, & God graunt me to do that thyng that may be to his pleasure. Amen.

Here speketh the auctour of suche as were most valiant imyghtis to be made mencion of in this boke. Capitulo II.

ALL noble hertis, to encorage & to shewe them ensample and mater of honour, I, Syr Johann Froissart begynne to speke after the true report and relation of my master Johan la Bele, somtyme Chanon of Saynte Lambertis of

experimental squares of grounding and gold as Morris tried out
recipes given in Theophilus and other ancient books. He compared the
methods of contemporary workers in gold and evolved his own
solution. One gets the impression that Morris's phases of technical
experimentation interested him almost more than the arrival. He once
showed his young daughters how the gold was laid, amusing them by
passing the broad badger gilding brush through his 'forest of thick
curls' like a hair brush before laying it gently on the leaf of gold. The
brush, slightly pre-greased by Morris's hair, took the gold leaf up
evenly, and transferred it to a little cushion for him to cut.

This passage, as well as being an intricate description of Morris at work, shows also the sympathy with his mind that makes this one of the great biographies.

The history of the founding of the Kelmscott Press is analogous to Fortuny's technical and aesthetic inventiveness with lighting. Morris was living in Kelmscott House in Hammersmith – named by him after Kelmscott Manor – and in 1891 he rented a cottage a few doors away to try 'turning printer'. The press later moved to larger premises nearby. Morris immersed himself in the printing process with his usual enthusiasm, designing new typefaces based on the calligraphy of the Middle Ages. He also needed to invent his own paper, modelled on a Bolognese paper made in 1473. This was shown to a paper manufacturer, Joseph Batchelor, who supplied three handmade papers for the

Kelmscott Press – Morris named the watermarks after English country things: Flower, Perch and Apple. MacCarthy tells us that on his first visit to Batchelor Morris 'could not resist taking his coat off and trying to make a sheet of paper. He succeeded at the second attempt'. A few copies were printed on vellum, and the books were bound in vellum and half holland. At first Morris obtained the vellum from Italy, but the entire production was then reserved by the Vatican. Morris found a British supplier and specified a vellum made from calfskin. He liked it to have a brownish cast and even a few hairs. The press published twenty-three of Morris's own books, many medieval texts, and books by poets Morris admired – Keats, Shelley, Tennyson and Swinburne – and the monumental Chaucer. As I have noted, it also published the handsome edition of Ruskin's chapter 'The Nature of Gothic' from *The Stones of Venice.*

The William Morris Museum in Walthamstow has some very interesting exhibits about the press and its workings. Indeed, this museum is both inventive and extremely interesting in its display of Morris's methods as well as of his finished work. It has excellent displays of Morris's work in many forms – including the archetypal wooden chairs sold by Morris & Co. It is in the house Morris lived in as a child, roaming the Essex woods, now, like the Red House, engulfed by outer London.

NORTH & SOUTH

Fortuny and Morris – Fortuny through Wagner – may both be said to have been interested in the myths, sagas and legends of the Nordic peoples. Fortuny went to Bayreuth in 1892 and came back deeply involved in Wagner's art, in the *Gesamtkunstwerk* Wagner proposed, combining acting, music, costume, lighting in one whole artwork. As Robert Donington brilliantly showed in *Wagner's 'Ring' and its Symbols* (1963), Wagner made formidably intelligent use both of the *Niebelungenlied* and of the tales in the Eddas and the Sagas, welding them together into one complex and tragic form. William Morris hated Wagner. In 1873, having returned from his second Icelandic journey, he wrote to the brother of Alfred Forman, who had sent him Forman's translation of Wagner's text of *Die Walküre*.

> *Many thanks for your letter and the translation of Wagner: I have not had time to read it yet: nor to say the truth am I much interested in anything Wagner does, as his theories on musical matters seem to me as an artist and non-musical man perfectly abhominable [sic]: besides I look upon it as nothing short of desecration to bring such a tremendous and world-wide subject under the gaslights of an opera: the most rococo and degraded of all forms of art – the idea of a sandy-haired German tenor tweedledeeing over the unspeakable woes of Sigurd, which even the simplest words are not typical enough to express! Excuse my heat but I wish to see Wagner uprooted, however clever he may be, and I don't doubt he is: but he is anti-artistic, don't doubt it.*

One of the motifs that both connects and separates Morris and Fortuny is the Wagnerian myth of Sigurd, Siegfried, the dragon and the ring. One bizarre contrast between my two heroes that amuses me is Morris's version of Fafnir the dragon compared to Fortuny's painting of the doomed incestuous lovers in the Valkyrie. Morris had an image of Fafnir, the terrible dragon or Worm. It was made of topiary – a yew hedge – and Morris had periodic dragon-trimming ceremonies with large shears. It is still at Kelmscott, perennially green. Whereas, on entering the salon in the Palazzo Fortuny (the Palazzo Pesaro Orfei), we see a painting made in 1928, *The Valkyrie, Siegmund and Sieglinde.* The background is very dark. We see the lovers in a tight embrace from behind; Sieglinde is clothed only in agitated transparent veiling. She is on tiptoe and the centre of the painting is the straining of her lovely buttocks against the shadowy dark male form whose dark arms clasp her naked shoulders. Fortuny invented what is still, I think, the most beautiful dress ever made for the female body – and he made it for many bodies, of many shapes.

Morris considered himself a man of the north, and during his lifetime translated many of the sagas from Icelandic with his friend Eiríkr Magnússon – amongst these *The Story of Grettir the Strong, Gunnlaug the Wormtongue* and the *Völsunga Saga* (the story of the Volsungs and Niblungs). Morris liked the harshness, cruelty and inevitability of stories like that of Gudrun, a beautiful and strong-minded woman who, when she finds out that she was tricked into marrying the friend of the man she loves, calls on her husband to kill her lover – which brings about her husband's own death. Morris's poem 'The Lovers of Gudrun' is in the last volume of *The Earthly Paradise*, and in the mid-1870s he published *The Story of Sigurd the Volsung*, a poem in four books, in long rhyming couplets. His long and ambitious work, *The Earthly Paradise*, published in four volumes between 1868 and 1870, is about a band of Norsemen, in the late fourteenth century, fleeing the Black Death and searching for the earthly Paradise 'where none grow old'. They end up on an island where the Greek gods are still worshipped, and ceremoniously exchange stories, the islanders from the classical mythology and epics, the Wanderers from the Norse, the Icelandic and medieval tales. This work was hugely popular in Morris's lifetime. It is also told in couplets, this time pentameters. I bought a vellum-bound edition from a bookstall in Cambridge in 1954 but I have never been able to read it for long – and even less *Sigurd the Volsung*. The rhythms hack and bang – I can read it best by 'hearing' Morris reading it aloud as he was in the habit of doing. But this poetry lives still – the contemporary Icelandic writer Sjón uses it in his novel *The Whispering Muse*, in which the same device of consecutive storytelling is used on board a Norwegian ship in a fjord, collecting wood to make paper. Sjón makes his own versions of the tales from *The Earthly Paradise*, and from Morris's *The Life and Death of Jason.* I said to Sjón that I loved Morris and wanted to read the epics, but that I found the verse forms unmanageable. He replied that they were indeed difficult, and needed

to be read a little at a time, but that Morris was a great man and a great writer, and we owed it to him to read him. It is good that he is being kept alive by an Icelander, for Iceland was Morris's vision of an essential part of his self.

He went there twice, once in 1871 and once in 1873. In 1871 he had just settled his family in Kelmscott, where Janey was with Rossetti and the daughters. His life was at a crisis point and he felt he needed the distance and harshness of the imagined wild. He travelled with Eiríkr Magnússon, his friend Charles Faulkner and a stranger, W. H. Evans, 'an officer and gentleman'. They made excursions on ponyback, and saw the volcanoes, the lava, the shores, the geysers. It was, as MacCarthy remarks, the kind of male adventure Morris liked – companionship and humour. Morris learned Icelandic from Magnússon, and became fluent. He wrote a splendid poem, 'Iceland First Seen'.

Lo from our loitering ship
a new land at last to be seen;
Toothed rocks down the side of the firth
on the east guard a weary wide lea,
And black slope the hillsides above,
striped adown with their desolate green:
And a peak rises up on the west
from the meeting of cloud and of sea,
Foursquare from base unto point

like the building of Gods that have been,
The last of that waste of the mountains
all cloud-wreathed and snow-flecked and grey,
And bright with the dawn that began
just now at the ending of day.

Ah! what came we forth for to see
that our hearts are so hot with desire?
Is it enough for our rest,
the sight of this desolate strand,
And the mountain-waste voiceless as death
but for winds that may sleep not nor tire?
Why do we long to wend forth
through the length and breadth of a land,
Dreadful with grinding of ice
and record of scarce hidden fire,
But that there 'mid the grey grassy dales
sore scarred by the ruining streams
Lives the tale of the Northland of old
and the undying glory of dreams?

Morris wrote a journal of this journey, which Geoffrey Grigson described as 'the best book of travel by an English poet ... which is also one of the least known'. Morris did not publish it in his lifetime.

The English poet Lavinia Greenlaw published an edition, with the title *Questions of Travel*, in 2011. She discerns in the journal Morris's attempt to connect with his own imagination through the harshness and pared-down simplicity of the landscape and the people's plain lives. He described the lava, the rare plants, the birds and fish. Here is an early description of the place, seen from the ship:

> on our left was a dark brown ragged island, Papey, and many small skerries about it, and beyond that we saw the mainland, a terrible shore indeed: a great mass of dark grey mountains worked into pyramids and shelves, looking as if they had been built and half ruined; they were striped with snow high up, and wreaths of cloud dragged across them here and there, and above them were two peaks and a jagged ridge of pure white snow ...

And here is Morris riding over the plain where the adventures of the sagas took place:

> As we ride along (over the lava now) we come opposite to a flat-topped hill some way down the lava stream, and just below it opens a huge black chasm, that runs straight away south towards the lake, a great double-walled dyke, but with its walls tumbled and ruined a good deal in places: the hill is Hrafnabjörg (Raven Burg) and the chasm Hrafnagjá (Raven Rift). But as we turn west we can see, a

long way off across the grey plain, a straight black line running from the foot of Armannsfell right into the lake, which we can see again hence and some way up from the lake a white line cuts the black one across. The black and white lines are the Almannagná (Great Rift) and the Öxará (Axe Water) tumbling over it. Once again that thin thread of insight and imagination which comes so seldom to us, and is such a joy when it comes, did not fail me at this first sight of the greatest marvel and most storied place of Iceland.

Morris was very fat and unfit when he set out. He was dismayed by having to ride a pony but found he enjoyed it, and he coped well

with the hard moments of the journey. Burne-Jones made a particularly cruel cartoon of Morris on a pony in Iceland. But Morris took the pony back to Kelmscott, where it became happily at home.

In 1878 Jane Morris and her daughters spent the winter with friends on the Italian Riviera, at Oneglia. Jenny Morris – who was affected by increasingly severe epilepsy – was seventeen. Their hostess, Rosalind Howard, reported that 'The M's are not quite so happy as I hoped they might be. Garden a perfect paradise but somehow the girls do not take so kindly to Italy as I hoped.' Fiona MacCarthy observes: 'May, evidently going through an awkward phase, announced one day that she would rather be in Iceland.' Morris's daughter was as fiercely northern as he was.

Fortuny's imagery and his mythology, in keeping with the photograph of him with beard and turban, are as southern as Morris's are northern. True, they share an interest in the matter of the *Niebelungenlied*, but Fortuny's passion for the tetralogy is part of a passion for art and artifice, for the *Gesamtkunstwerk*, for the intricacies of the theatre. Between December 2012 and April 2013 the Museo Fortuny had a rich exhibition: *Fortuny e Wagner: Il Wagnerismo nelle arte visive in Italia*. This showed Fortuny's work – both his paintings and his work on theatrical sets and lighting – in the context of a complex and varied Wagnerian interest in southern culture at the end of the nineteenth century and beginning of the twentieth. There were paintings by many other artists as well as Fortuny – Lionello Balestrieri, Leo Putz, Alois Delug, Teodoro Wolf Ferrari amongst them. Fortuny's own Wagner paintings are very interesting but gentler than Wagner himself. More exciting are some of the engravings, darker and tougher – Fafnir going off with the gold, Wotan striking the rock from which jet the flames that surround the Valkyrie, Mime the Nibelung seeking out soporific plants.

I have read that Fortuny always considered himself primarily a painter, and it was illuminating to see him in the context of his family of Spanish painters at an exhibition in New York, in 2012, at the Queen Sofía Spanish Institute. This exhibition showed some of the works of the Madrazo artistic dynasty, as well as Fortuny's own. There were paintings and drawings by his great-grandfather José de Madrazo, his grandfather Federico de Madrazo, and his uncle Raimundo de Madrazo, who was a close friend and sometime collaborator of Fortuny's father, Fortuny y Marsal. After Fortuny y Marsal's early death, Raimundo became influential in his nephew's education. The New York exhibition showed paintings by these men, comprising both sun-drenched southern landscapes and gardens, and Arab clothing and *objets d'art*. There were wonderful paintings by Fortuny y Marsal and Raimundo de Madrazo of the garden of the Fortuny residence, *c.*1872 and 1877, showing tall, still yews or cedars, a still path and an elegant white-gowned woman with a scarlet parasol and a fan, strolling peacefully. There was a painting by Raimundo de Madrazo of *The Pavilion of Carlos V in the Gardens*

of the Alcazar of Seville (1868), with the same mixture of bright sun and sharp shade, stillness and quiet – a red-robed figure is seated talking to a gardener, in front of a carved wall and a terrace, and in the foreground is a group of animated small pecking birds, a watering can and a rake. There were also paintings by Fortuny y Marsal of beautifully observed Moroccans, and an animated almost grotesque etching of a snake charmer, lying on a carpet and watched by a tall stork-like bird. Federico studied dress in Egypt and elsewhere, and made elaborate records of costumes and clothes. The great-grandfather José de Madrazo painted classical dramas, travelled to Rome to study ancient ruins and art, and held the view, the art historian José Luis Diez noted, that 'ancient Greece was the real classical civilisation, Rome being no more than a pale copy'. Fortuny y Marsal collected objects, according to Guillermo de Osma, 'tapestries, Japanese armour, Hispano-Moresque weapons and ceramics, and ceramics, fabrics, paintings'. Fortuny was continuing a tradition, or several connected traditions, although he was also, as a designer, striking out on his own. In his turn he travelled to Africa and to Greece, making paintings and taking photographs of Morocco and Egypt, Greece and Crete, the Parthenon and street Moroccans. In 2004 the Museo Fortuny and the Civic Museums of Venice put on an exhibition of Fortuny's photographs from a journey he made with Henriette, in 1938, to Egypt.[*]

---

[*] *Mariano Fortuny. Viaggio in Egitto. Appunti fotografici d'artista.* Venice, Palazzo Fortuny/ Fondazione Musei Civici di Venezia, 2004.

He was an excellent photographer, particularly of simple scenes of ordinary people, lives and buildings.

If Morris and his contemporaries were possessed by the medieval Christian imagination and the ancient sagas, the moderns looked further back to the ancient world, and rewrote the Greek myths and legends to suit their own ideas about society and history. Fortuny's work is intimately involved in this modernist rethinking, most particularly of the Cretan civilisation in Knossos, and the imagination of a 'Minoan' dynasty, as opposed to the Achaeans of mainland Greece. Heinrich Schliemann made various attempts in the 1870s to discover and dig up the remains of Troy. There is an excellent account of Schliemann's discoveries, 'theories', fantasies and myths in Cathy Gere's fascinating book *Knossos and the Prophets of Modernism*, to which I am much indebted. Schliemann invented Germanic theories about Troy and the buried treasure of Priam and the body of Agamemnon. He played with ideas of an Aryan civilisation, and used the symbolism of the swastika, a faked image of which appeared on the vulva of a lead figurine of a goddess, *Ilios*. Schliemann's work was taken up by German Nationalist movements, as they elaborated the idea of racial purity, Aryan civilisation and particularly the symbolism of the swastika.

There was also an alternative story of a matriarchal civilisation. In 1861 Johann Jakob Bachofen, a Swiss antiquarian, jurist and anthropologist, published *Das Mutterrecht*, in which he described a cultural history in four phases: Hetairism, the Mutterrecht, the

Dionysian and the Apollonian. Hetairism was an early nomadic phase, 'communistic and polyamorous.' Its god was an early earthy Aphrodite. This was followed by the Mutterrecht, a matriarchal society, dominated by a version of Demeter the earth goddess, in which Bachofen discerned chthonic mystery cults and the emergence of law. This was followed by the Dionysian and the emergence of patriarchy, which was in turn followed by the modern Apollonian (and masculine) civilisation.

These ideas, and other similar ones, influenced another myth-maker and archaeologist, the British Arthur Evans, who excavated Minoan Crete. Evans shared Schliemann's enthusiasm, creativity and propensity to alter and even to fake the archaeological evidence. He made his own ferrous concrete structure of the palace of Knossos, obscuring much evidence forever. But the myths he invented were more sympathetic than Schliemann's. His Minos was not an evil king with a dreadful minotaur hidden in a labyrinth – he was a wise and just ruler of a peaceful and prosperous nation. Cathy Gere tells us that in the beginning Evans was obsessed with Ariadne, she who had held the thread which led out of the labyrinth. Gere writes:

> *His first gesture was to place her on the throne of the palace,*
> *suggesting that Crete had been one of the last outposts of a*
> *once-universal, matriarchal stage of human cultural evolution. She*
> *didn't last too long as the ruler of Knossos, but Evans compensated*

for her loss of temporal power by anointing her the queen of the
Minoan heaven, the Great Mother Goddess of an ecstatic nature
religion practiced on the mountaintops and in the sacred groves of
the island. Above all it was her legendary 'dancing floor' that he
would return to as a symbolic location that united the deep past
with his fondest hopes for the present and future of Crete.

Evans returned again and again to the dancing girls and those who were bull-leapers. He compared them to modern women – in one wall painting he described them as like beauties painted by Toulouse-Lautrec, 'fresh from the coiffeur's hand with hair *frisé* and curled about the head and shoulders'. Evans quoted the *Iliad*'s description of Achilles' shield, 'a dancing floor like the one Daedalus made at Knossos for Ariadne' 'where beautiful young men and girls are circling, touching each other's hands, the girls in garlands of flowers and soft linens, the men sporting gold-hilted daggers'.

Another theorist of feminist culture in Knossos was the British scholar Jane Harrison, a Fellow of Newnham College in Cambridge, who visited Evans, worked on the excavations and wrote about the Minoan civilisation. In her most famous book, *Prolegomena to the Study of Greek Religion* (1903), there is a chapter called 'The Making of a Goddess' in which, Gere says, 'hundreds of coded references to the traumatic transition from matriarchy to patriarchy could be detected in legend, ritual, relief and vase painting'. The story was a bitter one.'Woman who was the inspirer, becomes the temptress; she who made all things, god and mortals alike, is become their plaything, their slave, dowered only with physical beauty, and with a slave's tricks and blandishments.' Harrison returned to the theme in *Themis* (1912), in which she describes the sacrifice of a bull to Dionysus, painted on the sides of a Minoan sarcophagus. 'In the centre we have the sacrifice of a bull ... He is dying not dead; his tail is still alive and his pathetic eyes wide open, but the flute player is playing and the blood flows from the bull's neck ...'

Mariano Fortuny read Arthur Evans's *The Prehistoric Tombs of Knossos* in 1906. He made notes on this book and wrote: 'In 1907 some printed fragments of cloth found in Greece encouraged me to conduct research on printing procedures from the past, after which my wife and I started a workshop in Palazzo Pesaro Orfei to put into practice the methods we had discovered'. Ilaria Caloi has written a very interesting article, 'The reception of the Minoans in the modern art of Mariano Fortuny y Madrazo', in which she explains that Fortuny's interest in Minoan art – as opposed to Aegean – is specific and unusual. Fortuny also read Angelo Mosso, the Italian archaeologist, who wrote *Escursioni nel Mediterraneo*. Caloi has studied Fortuny's papers collected in the Museo Fortuny and quotes him on Knossos.

Quando tornai a Venezia fui indotto a ricercare gli antichi metodi della stampa su stoffe. Le scoperti fatte da Angelo Mosso su Creta furono di grande incentivo a tentare alcune prove. E il primo saggio

fu una sciarpa dipinta, una sciarpa lunga, che chiamai appunto
Knossòs dai motivi di fiore e alghe che corrono intorno agli
antichissimi vasi ritrovati nell'isola di Candia.

When I returned to Venice, I was prompted to research the ancient
methods of textile printing. Angelo Mosso's findings on Crete were a
great incentive to attempt some pieces. And the first experiment was
a painted scarf, a long scarf, which I named Knossos after the
flower and seaweed patterns that run around the very ancient vases
uncovered on the island of Candia.

Fortuny went twice to Greece but never to Crete. The first Knossos
scarf was made in 1907. There are splendid photographs of Henriette
wrapped in one. The scarves had a coin-shaped stamp on one corner
depicting a labyrinth. He used, Caloi tells us, 'Minoan themes such
as landscapes with plants and flowers, marine environments with
seaweeds and animals, like octopuses, argonauts and murex shells'.
He used an ancient Cretan image of lilies, surprisingly modern even
today. The scarves were hugely successful, and in 1909 Fortuny
patented his other great success, the pleated Delphos, based on the
robes seen on male and female Greek statues such as the Kore of
Euthydikos, the Kore of Samos and the Charioteer of Delphi. He
worked initially with a drawing of the charioteer Henriette had made
on an earlier Greek journey. The Delphos was – to quote the

description given to register the trademark in Paris – a 'sheath open at both ends, gathered at the top in such a way as to form a neck opening at the centre; with two openings for the arms on either side, two openings with hems tightened by laces along the arms, and slanting draw hems for adjusting the sleeves'. The sheaths could have long, short or no sleeves. These simple, complex and wonderful garments were held together with Venetian Murano glass beads, the only part of the dresses – apart from the original silk – that was not made in the Fortuny palazzo and later dye-works. There was also the Peplos, named for the uneven-hemmed overgarment worn by the Kore of Samos, and a great variety of overgarments, transparent or made of rich brocades and velvets.

Fortuny applied for a patent for this new 'invention' at the Office National de la Propriété Industrielle in Paris in 1909. The dresses were made of fine silk which was imported from Japan and China. When, later, Mussolini declared that only Italian resources were to be used, Fortuny had to ask for help from the American Elsie McNeill, who became Elsie Lee, and later still the Contessa Gozzi. Lee helped him with the sales and distribution of his work in the States and elsewhere. She was able to purvey the silk to him by circuitous methods. Writers on Fortuny say that the method used to produce the permanent pleats is still a mystery. There were hundreds of pleats around each dress and they were all made by hand. Guillermo de Osma gives us a description.

The method needed a lot of manual work, since the folds are all different and irregular. They were probably put into the material when it was wet, perhaps still under water, with heat being applied later to ensure that they remained permanent. During the latter process it is possible that a piece of thread may have been passed through each group of pleats in order to tighten them for a time.

The patent included a method of undulating the material horizontally once it had been pleated. To undulate the silk he designed a system of horizontally placed copper or porcelain tubes that could be heated from within. The pleated piece of silk, still wet, would be placed between these tubes, and the permanently undulating effect created by the heat.

Fortuny searched widely for his dyes – like Morris returning to ancient and subtle vegetable dyes. His dye-works can still be visited on the Giudecca, like Morris's in Merton Abbey. He was inventive with the ways he printed his designs. He studied printing on fabrics, substituting the wooden blocks used to print dyes on silk in the early days of the Knossos with ones made of metal that allowed him to overlap several colours on a single decorative motif. He also collected Japanese *katagami* stencils and studied their methods and use. Henriette worked with him on all these operations. Indeed, one source says that the original idea for the form of the Delphos was hers – after her drawing of the

Charioteer of Delphos. They made velvet coats and cloaks, and simple, elegant handbags to go with the pocketless dresses. The gowns were sold wound into spirals in specially designed boxes.

Mary Lydon, in her book *Skirting the Issue*, has a very interesting discussion of Proust's study of Fortuny and what Fortuny meant to him. Fortuny is first mentioned in *À la recherche* by Elstir, the painter, and Lydon develops Proust's image of the artist as couturier. This connects to the alternative images of the novel as a dress, and the novel as a cathedral, studied by Butor. Lydon forms a theory – supported by good evidence – that Proust thought of his own writing as something made with pleats – folds, *plis*. She has her own take on the idea of the Fortuny gown as a liberation of the female body. She points out tartly that although Fortuny's garments were said to be designed to free women from the constrictions of whalebone, they in fact restricted women's movements in another way, by insisting that the hemlines should extend for four to six inches beyond the toes of the wearer, impeding her walking and making her appear 'rooted to the spot'.

Fortuny's work excited other artists, including writers. D'Annunzio, in a novel begun in 1908 (*Forse che sì, forse che no*), was already describing the Knossos worn by his heroine.

> *She was wrapped in one of those very long scarves of oriental gauze*
> *that the alchemist dyer Mariano Fortuny steeps in the mysterious*
> *recesses of his vats, which are stirred with a wooden spear, now by*

a sylph, now by a hobgoblin, and he draws them out coloured
with strange dreamlike shades, and then he prints on them with
a thousand blows of his burnishing tool new generations of stars,
plants and animals. Surely with Isabella Inghirani's scarf he must
have suffused the dye with a small amount of the pink stolen by
his sylph from a rising moon.

There are other literary accounts of Fortuny's garments which immediately were understood as modern (timeless) works of art and exhibited in galleries and museums as such. I found an interesting attitude to Fortuny's work in a 'fashion memoir' (in a series of memoirs about great figures of fashion) by Delphine Desvaux. She herself is not wholly enthusiastic about Fortuny – she finds him not to be a couturier and asserts that literature has treated Fortuny harshly, which is clearly not the case. She cites D'Annunzio's novel – not the ecstatic description of the dress but the moment when its wearer 'overcome by misery, later abandons one of her dresses in her flight; it is left hanging on the end of her bed, a pathetic sloughed skin'. Desvaux also describes a scene in Proust where the narrator sees Oriane de Guermantes 'wrapped in a Fortuny-type kimono dressing-gown, the colour of a butterfly's wing ... she certainly looks very beautiful.' But the narrator does not find her desirable and pointedly refers to the unpleasant smell of her dress (caused by the Chinese crystallised egg-white used as a fixative by Fortuny).

Fortuny's dresses can be seen in the wider context of the reform of women's dress at the turn of the century. In late Victorian times the movement for 'rational dress' set out to liberate women from constricting corsets, innumerable buttons, tight waists and gripping brassieres. The simple dresses worn by Janey Morris were an aspect of this way of seeing things. The paintings of Frederic Leighton, Sir Lawrence Alma-Tadema, Albert Moore and John William Godward showed women in Greek classical flowing gowns, and were exhibited in Venice at the Biennale where they were seen by Fortuny, who also knew the aesthetic tea gowns sold by Liberty in London. Fortuny's dresses were exhibited in New York in 1914, and in 1916 Belle Armstrong Whitney used his gowns as an example of 'ideal dress' in *What to Wear: A Book for Women*, saying she believed Fortuny's gowns fulfilled all her conditions for the ideal dress, which should be above fashion and change: 'efficiency, simplicity, personality, quality materials and a high standard of workmanship and artistry'. Fortuny's early gowns were designed to be worn without underwear, and the wearers were expected to wear them in private as tea gowns, or a kind of negligee. But they made their way into the larger world and were worn by women of fashion in many countries and most particularly by dancers and actresses.

Perhaps the commercial and aesthetic success of Fortuny's clothes came more from his work as a theatrical designer than from any close connection to haute couture. The American dancer Ruth

St Denis wore Fortuny's Knossos scarf for performances of 'Indian' dances in Berlin in 1907. Both Isadora Duncan and Eleanora Duse wore Fortuny dresses to dance. Cathy Gere tells an arresting tale of a visit by Isadora Duncan to Knossos in 1910: 'upon sighting the four completed flights of the grand staircase' she 'could not contain herself and threw herself into one of her impromptu dances for which she was so well known. Up and down the steps she danced, her dress flowing around her.' Gere records that the site supervisor was shocked and goes on:

> What the notoriously woman-shy Mackenzie failed to appreciate was how fashionably appropriate Duncan's anachronisms were. As she whirled up and down the grand staircase with her bare toes and her wispy garb – her dancing amply supported by the strength of ferro-concrete – she perfectly embodied the Dionysian significance of the reconstructions. Here was a place where the most outlandish expressions of post-Nietzschean enthusiasm for the modernity of the Greek spirit could find expression, and where liberated femininity (clad in the folds and pleats of Duncan's completely un-Minoan 'Greek' costume) could insinuate itself into the new tragic age.

A silk scarf was also the occasion of Duncan's own tragic death, as it floated from her neck, in an open car, and tangled itself irretrievably in the hub of a wheel. This scarf was not a Knossos but was a painted silk scarf by the Russian-born artist Roman Chatov.

FABRICS, DESIGNS & LIGHT

When I began to write this essay I had a very simplified concept of the contrast of the designs of the two artists. My favourite images by Morris are his Honeysuckle and his Willow Boughs, both of which show how accurately Morris had observed the growing forms of the plants at Kelmscott. I remember being overcome with delight when I first realised how rigorously the geometry of plants worked among the apparently accidental forms of particular flowers or leaves. There are plants which grow according to the Fibonacci spiral – 1, 1, 2, 3, 5, 8, etc. – which always seemed to me a peculiarly human construction – each number being the sum of the previous two numbers – and not a growth pattern at all. In the Honeysuckle and the Willow Boughs the feeling of free growth is contained in the geometrical repetitions. (We have the Morris willow leaves in our living room – they are surprisingly happy with modern paintings.) Morris said that images of plants should strive upwards and onwards, towards spaces beyond the painting or cloth.

I saw Fortuny equally simply, as an artist who made intricate designs of all shapes and sizes but without Morris's belief in movement and 'drive'. His imagery derived from all sorts of ancient and medieval designs, in the buildings of Venice, on the splendid fabrics in his mother's chest. He was working with, and adding to, and changing, a long history of human images of growing things – vines, acanthus leaves, pomegranates – which had symbolic meanings in the Christian religion. Reading Fortuny and Morris together made me think very hard, and with great pleasure, about the need to make representations of the outside world, and about the need to hand these on and change them.

I have made many discoveries during the writing of this essay, which began with my instinctive closing of my eyes on the dark inside of Fortuny's palace, and on a world of waterways and stone, in order to see, with my inner eye, the green and flowery world of Kelmscott, near its own unostentatious river. Following this apparently haphazard contrast has led to all sorts of surprising juxtapositions of the two men and the two worlds, and to unexpected new understanding. Most of all, perhaps, in the things they made – and of these, most of all in the textiles.

Where to begin? Looking at Fortuny's designs and comparing them to Morris's makes me see just how much Morris was ill at ease, with the human certainly, but also with the animal in general. His sense of failure when he painted Janey's portrait – 'I cannot paint you but I love you' – was already part of him. As a boy he wasn't interested in art – he was interested in woods and water and wild flowers and the shapes of stones and currents. He not only couldn't draw men and women, he couldn't draw animals, from lions to rabbits. Images I had thought were his – in tapestries and printed cloths – were in fact done cooperatively by Philip Webb or by Burne-Jones. At some point in his history as an artist, as far as I can see, he set himself to learn how to draw animals and birds, though not human beings – his work begins to be more frequently attributed to him – though The

Firm continued to work together. And his representative work – even in highly stylised repetitive forms in wallpapers or carpets – seems, compared to other artists, as though the first impulse was to record something seen or noted. As he grew cleverer he elaborated the forms of flowers, and mixed one size of floret or bud with something incompatibly huger or smaller that is nevertheless part of the same design. He mixed one kind of trailing vegetable with a bunch of rounded petals and made us see both differently.

In a lecture of 1881, 'Some Hints on Pattern Designing', he spoke of the relations between design and real things.

> *Of course you understand that it is impossible to imitate nature literally; the utmost literalism of the most realistic painter falls a long way short of that … If you are to put nothing on it but what strives to be a literal imitation of nature, all you can do is to have a few cut flowers or bits of boughs nailed to it, with perhaps a blue-bottle fly or a butterfly here and there. – Is it not better to be reminded, however simply, of the close vine-trellis that keeps out the sun by the Nile side; or of the wild-woods and their streams, with the dogs panting beside them; or of the swallows sweeping above the garden boughs towards the house-eaves where their nestlings are, while the sun breaks the clouds on them; or of the many-flowered summer meadows of Picardy? Is not all this better than having to count day after day a few sham-real boughs and flowers casting*

sham-real shadows on your walls with little hint of anything beyond
Covent Garden in them?... Ornamental pattern-work ... must possess
three qualities: beauty, imagination and order ... as to the third –
order invents certain beautiful and natural forms, which will remind
not only of nature but also of much that lies beyond that part.

Morris went on to speak of the change, when classic structures were replaced by 'young Gothic', to the use of the continuous line, representing continuous growth. He made his own claims for representative content in the patterns.

I, as a Western man and a picture-lover, must still insist on plenty
of meaning in your patterns; I must have unmistakeable
suggestions of gardens and fields, and strange trees, boughs and
tendrils, or I can't do with your pattern, but must take the first piece
of nonsense-work a Kurdish shepherd has woven from tradition and
memory; all the more, as even in that there will be some hint
of past history.

If Morris believed in a necessary representative element in fabric design, his sense of the structures and forms he preferred was equally strong. He wanted clarity of form, and he had a need for growth and strength in his patterns. They must be going somewhere.

Above all things, avoid vagueness. Definite form bounded by firm outline is a necessity for all ornament ... do not be afraid of your design or try to muddle it up so that people can scarce see it; if it is arranged on good lines, and its details are beautiful, you need not fear its looking hard, so long as it covers the ground well and is not wrong in colour.

Rational growth is necessary to all patterns, or at least the hint of such growth; and in recurring patterns, at least, the noblest are those where one thing grows visibly and necessarily from another. Take heed in this growth that each member of it be strong and crisp, that the lines do not get thready or flabby or too far from their stock to sprout firmly and vigorously; even where a line ends it should look as if it had plenty of capacity for more growth if so it would.

Morris believed in the originality of the craftsman designer – don't copy any style, he said, but make your own – and then he added something perhaps unexpected –'yet you must study the history of our art' – and finished by joking about the trade.

If I am speaking to any pattern-designers here ... I should like to remind them of one thing, that the constant designing of recurring patterns is a very harassing business ... A friend of mine, who is a

Manchester calico-printer told me the other day that the shifty and clever designers who draw the thousand and one ingenious and sometimes pretty patterns for garment-goods which Manchester buys of Paris, have a tendency to go mad, and often do so; and I cannot wonder at it.

Fiona MacCarthy describes Morris in the 1870s working in what was then the South Kensington Museum, 'examining historic textiles, especially the Italian late-medieval patterns'. 'He was building up his own collection of samples: he lists at this period four pieces of brocatelle, *c.*1520', 'very curious and valuable', 'a collections of cut velvets, 'various dates from about 1560', a lady's jacket, 'knitted green silk and gold, pretty', 'scraps of a fine piece of gold cloth'. He studied plants and birds, both in historical collections and in his own garden and orchard. May Morris wrote in her biography of her father that he designed forty-five wallpapers and six ceiling papers, giving us an idea of the speed and energy with which he worked. In addition there were many fabric, tapestry and embroidery designs. Morris studied intently the relationship between the design and the fabric or paper where it would be installed – would there be movement, would the design be flat and still as in wallpapers or carpets? He produced designs in 1864, and again in 1868 when he designed five more papers and a chintz. Then another gap until 1871. His most energetic designing lasted until 1890 and the beginning

of his period of fierce political activity.

His late complex and costly design, Wild Tulip, created in 1884, derived from the Islamic designs from Turkey and Persia he studied in the museum. He was thinking about the explosion of images of tulips made by Dutch and Flemish painters in the seventeenth century, when the flower was designed and redesigned and became inordinately expensive. He was also thinking about the Near Eastern tulips in the garden in Kelmscott which flourished energetically.

Like Morris, Fortuny came relatively late to the design of textiles – he was influenced by his work in theatre design, and by his passion for Wagner. His most important works, the Knossos shawl and the pleated Delphos dress, were made at the beginning of the twentieth century. If Morris was excited by natural places, growths and creatures, Fortuny was moved by women. Most of all, of course, by his wife, Henriette, who worked with him on the design and construction of the fabrics, and modelled them. There are photographs of women wearing nothing but a completely transparent shift – 'made in transparent ochre silk gauze, printed in silver with plant motifs and worn next the skin'. They are exquisitely beautiful and graceful, but they are not sexy, either in 1910 or now. Apparently the Delphos dresses were made all the same size, with possibilities for adjusting their length and width for different women. The models are, it seems to me, mostly photographed with bare feet beneath the extravagantly long hems.

Fortuny's dresses seem to represent two starkly different things. They are made of silk or velvet, in a huge variety of brilliant, subtle colours. They descend simply over the body and end in a pool of shimmering light. They are worn over naked flesh, or over a silk shift. Their simplicity is more glamorous than most high couture designs. At the same time they are in a curious way *comfortable*. Women may relax in them, lying in an armchair or on a couch, and the pleats may be rucked up, and the wearer may be plump or tiny or tall, and she will look at home in her simple garment. They were worn by princesses and grand dames, by Isadora Duncan and Peggy Guggenheim. Susan Sontag was buried in a Fortuny, as was the heroine of Mary McCarthy's novel *The Group* – making some sort of statement about life, death and enduring beauty. The dresses were shown at the Venice Biennale. Fortuny was an artist, and he saw his dresses as works of art. He refused to make a dress for Rita Hayworth – reminding me of a later artist who made splendidly simple clothes, Jean Muir, who refused to design for Margaret Thatcher.

I have been told more than once that there was nothing original in Fortuny's designs – he simply copied motifs from old church vestments and furniture designs. This criticism was obviously made in his lifetime – in 1910 when he took out a second patent to protect his printing technique that gives velvet an embossed effect found in old brocades, he issued a disclaimer.

The aim of the Société Anonyme Fortuny has never been to create a false antique. In other words, the fabrics are not 'imitations of the old'. They are re-editions that are interpreted or translated, as it were, into another language, printed instead of woven, with beautiful patterns drawing on all epochs and all genres. At times they take after fragments of precious fabrics, at times they are completely original. Other times the designs are completely new and modern creations.

And when one comes to look at Fortuny's work, over time and in detail, the idea of 'originality' and the idea of 'derivation' seem somehow beside the point. Fortuny was making studies, working out themes and ideas, from many cultures and in many colours and forms, new and old, combined in new ways or presented in new contexts. Where Morris went back to living creatures and growing plants, Fortuny's world was human, layer upon layer, intertwined and intersecting. De Osma remarks that the motifs from Arab and North African cultures should be seen as Fortuny's own inheritance through his father. He lists some – fifteenth-century vegetable motifs that came to Europe from Persia and Turkey, European textiles of the seventeenth, eighteenth and nineteenth centuries, 'as well as many motifs from Cretan, Arabic (epigraphic textiles), Indian, Chinese, Japanese and later pre-Colombian and Oceanic (Maori) art'. Some of his strikingly 'modern' linear geometric designs turn out to originate in ancient

Central America. And there are surprises – a design based on repeated, regular images of fossil trilobites, and another, cotton satin in a goldish colour, with a motif in silver metal that looks, with twining stems and flickering leaves, just like a tribute to Morris's Willow Boughs.

And always there were the churches of Venice, and the paintings, above all by Carpaccio, in those churches. This is a world of hangings, upholsteries, huge curtains, rich military garments, sweeping silk capes beside stone stairs and landings and the ever-present water. Fortuny was a naturalist, of a different kind from Morris, in his photographs, showing not well-known 'views' but mostly narrow alleys, and secretive looking posts, and the backs of women carrying burdens in the streets. As a photographer he is also a naturalist – he records the life of the streets, and the weather over the canals, creating surprising panoramas, and lights and shadows.

De Osma observes that Fortuny was possessed by the Nordic and found it hard to shake off. He was possessed by Wagner, and by the idea of the *Gesamtkunstwerk*. De Osma quotes an amazing passage – he says it is illustrating Fortuny's preference for 'less complicated and sensational scenes' – but I think Fortuny is writing about the aesthetic experience of Wagner's leitmotifs.

Fortuny writes:

> *It is possible to have a work created in an instant that may completely satisfy the intellect of its author ... in which case, either it*

represents a long period of intellectual work, or it becomes a 'motif'
no more or less than a product of nature. Sublime art, such as that
of Wagner or Michelangelo, is extremely rich in motifs, so much so
that any fragment of their works, however small, is as large as any
other, because it offers a motif, and whatever that may be, whether
the wing of a mosquito or an enormous mountain, in no way will
the one be greater than the other.

When I read this – the latest of many readings – I associated it for the first time with the motifs in the textiles – pomegranates, lilies, peacocks, rabbits, strawberries, gryphons, stars. At the beginning of writing this essay, I saw the images of textiles whole, remembering perhaps a colour and a rhythm, the distance of one shape from another. Then I began to look closely at the motifs – what sort of pomegranate is this? How does it relate, spatially and in colour, to the other images? Is it simply elegant or flaunting or there for the visual rhythm? And then I began to think about human history, and how humans decided to make representations of pomegranates (for instance) and why, and did these images acquire allegorical or metaphysical meanings, and when, and who could read them, in a church window, or on a silk dress or a velvet coat?

POMEGRANATE

The pomegranate has symbolised life, death and the borders between the two in many cultures and at many times. Ancient Egyptians were buried with pomegranates as images of a new life. Pomegranates were embroidered on the hems of the robes of Hebrew High Priests, and grew in Islam's four gardens of Paradise. Robert Browning's mysterious title for his poems, *Bells and Pomegranates*, refers to these priestly hems. They were blessed fruits to Buddhists – ripe, open pomegranates were symbols of fertility and plenty. Anglo-Saxons probably know best the classical myth of Proserpina or Persephone, daughter of Ceres (Demeter in Greek) who was the goddess of earth and fertility. She was swept away by Pluto (Dis), god of the underworld, to be his consort and sit beside him on his dark throne. Her distraught mother neglected the earth, everything decayed and died, and Zeus was forced to ask Pluto to restore her. This turned out to be only partially possible, because Proserpina's return depended on her having eaten nothing in the underworld, whereas she had been tempted to eat four pomegranate seeds. So she had to return to the underworld for four months a year, our winter months. This pomegranate is lusciously and equivocally portrayed in Dante Gabriel Rossetti's painting of Janey Morris – entitled *Proserpine* – where the beautiful woman is dark and brooding and holds up the sliced fruit displaying the juicy seeds. A cruel interpretation would suggest that Mrs Morris is doomed to spend a dark wintry life with her husband, with only a glimpse of fruit and light (and Rossetti). The painting hung in the dining room at Kelmscott.

I cannot imagine that Morris – however charitable – enjoyed it.

William Morris first undertook to represent pomegranates in 1864 – he produced a design for 'fruit' or 'pomegranates' which originally also contained some elegant olive branches. Like many designs by Morris the original identity is dubious – is it a fruit, is it a pomegranate? It is oval in shape, rather than round, and looks unlike any pomegranate I have ever seen. It was designed a decade before Rossetti's painting, and the geometry combines the tile shapes he had been working on, with the slanting boughs of the tree. The 'fruit' are more like lemons, ovals with spotted skins that come to a point, though there are also some round shapes with two cheeks. Later designs with pomegranates are realistic, rounded and convincing, some burst open to show the bright red seeds, some still clamped shut. And there is a splendid fabric designed by John Henry Dearle, who was Morris's former pupil, who had a long and distinguished career as head designer at Morris & Co. Some of Dearle's work rivals Morris's own, and his designs are scrupulous, delicate and surprising. His Bird and Pomegranate is still on sale, with various alternative background colours, and has the intricacy of Dearle at his best. It has intertwining branches, not unlike willow boughs, and is spangled with fruit, split open at inviting angles to reveal the red ripe shiny seeds. The boughs are also inhabited by small birds, red-capped like the red pomegranates, or soft grey, flying in to peck at unopened fruit, or by tiny soft grey birds pecking at other fruit. Dearle was very good at depicting many varieties of English birds

from many points of view. His design is very orderly and complicated if worked out, but looks happily random at first sight.

Rossetti's pomegranate is both mythical and personal. Morris's, like most of his work, is at one level, the most important level, a representation of a living and growing creature. Fortuny is different. He is working within an accepted symbolism and an accepted gathering of forms, which he plays with, and extends and changes. To begin with, I did not particularly notice pomegranates. Now I see that, in Fortuny, they are everywhere, a language of motifs, as he said himself. It is interesting that Fortuny's mother's first purchase for her collection of fabrics was 'a blood-red piece of old velvet, embellished by pomegranates'.

Describing 'a sixteenth-century-style red textile' illustrated in her book, Deschodt describes richness in order. The textile 'alternates branches with three artichokes and three pomegranates to form a reticulate repeat with ogival links. In the centre of each ogive is a thistle framed by raspberry bushes, or a pinecone nestled in pomegranate flowers. The Spanish-Moorish border has vine tendrils interspersed with leaves.' Fortuny turned to many times and cultures – Byzantine, Venetian, Renaissance Italian, Greek, Japanese, Indian, Egyptian and Far Eastern, seventeenth- and eighteenth-century France, and in most of these pomegranates can be found, endlessly similar, endlessly variable. They can be combined with thistles – both plants symbolised fertility and abundance in the Near and Middle East, and fabrics with these

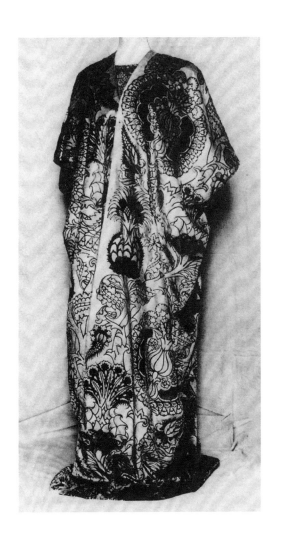

designs were made from the fifteenth to the seventeenth centuries when Italy traded with the Ottoman Empire. Both pomegranate and thistle have a rounded seed container surmounted by a crown of leaves. They can suggest a closed secret, or something about to burst with shining crimson seeds, with lifeblood in birth and death. The pomegranate was used to adorn images of the crucifixion and resurrection of Christ. Fortuny copies these images, turns them on their sides, redesigns them or makes new images of his own. Pomegranates stand at the centre of a design, or run in ribbons of repeated forms as an ornament. I should like to know if Fortuny, when designing a gown, or a cope, or a velvet cape, thought of the meaning of the images, or just of their traditional and satisfactory beauty.

Once I started looking closely for them in Fortuny's work I found page after page of different pomegranates, which slot into place in the brain as a complicated pattern once one is alerted to them. There are stylised fat pomegranates like stolid onions in a bracelet of flowers in gold-printed silk velvets, dyed with cochineal. There are Renaissance and other patterns on velvet, with large amphorae between volutes of acanthus, from which spring vine tendrils bearing pomegranates, pears and a large tulip. Others have Islamic decorative features, including the Rumi leaf. There is a delicious fifteenth-century delicate cotton with twining pink linear forms, branchlets ending in pomegranates, sinuous pink branches like snakes ending in thistles grasping the pomegranates, and a central pomegranate, realistic and onion-solid, surrounded by a circle of solid pink florets. Fortuny used a small motif on a faded blue ground, which 'may be seen in fabrics worn by figures in Renaissance paintings, especially those of Piero della Francesca' (Doretta Davanzo Poli). Here the stone-coloured pomegranates sprout in threes from a branch curiously and formally knotted with human handmade knots. Fortuny, like his mother, collected fabrics and used old ones as inspiration – he collected fragments of old Cretan printed cloths, and copied the designs.

Fortuny made rich designs for church garments, for grandes dames and for bishops, for funerals and for dancers and actors onstage. His copes gave prominent place to pomegranates. A bishop's cope made of gold-printed scarlet velvet, with patterns adapted from fifteenth-century church vestments, is rich with pomegranates of varying sizes – a huge one in the middle of the back, large ones – dissimilar in design – below it, with red flowers sprouting from the round, pointed-leaf-coated base. When you look carefully there are more and more pomegranates – tiny ones in groups of three, amongst curls of acanthus leaves. Fortuny invented ways of adding new metallic colours to his fabrics, effects of silver and gold, without using the metals themselves. There is a particularly splendid cope, made in 1936, in a dark silk velvet, with an encircled outline of a golden pomegranate in the middle of the shoulders at the back, beneath which is a design of ordered chaos, curling seawaves or acanthus leaves, richly golden, with thin curling tendrils inside the curl of the leaf. There is (to a British eye) nothing specifically religious about what is being celebrated – just beauty and growth.

He spread the pomegranate on a long court mantle, in gold- and silver-printed velvet, trimmed and lined with fur, in a Renaissance style, with woody branches rising solidly up the back of the garment, bearing slimmer branches thick with fat pomegranates, bristling with spines, bursting with fruit, using the long upward space to splendid effect.

If the pomegranate was used religiously as a symbol of plenty, of life within death, the fruit could also be used to imply and to decorate the female body, rich, promising, fertile. Fortuny used it frequently.

There is a long coat in the Museo Fortuny of which I have only seen small black-and-white photographs. It is described as having a 'pomegranate motif of Renaissance inspiration'. It is covered with bold pomegranate images with fanned-out feathery tops – what struck me was that there is a very fat pomegranate sited where the coat-sides meet, and just at the most delicate part of the female anatomy. I've seen more than one of these photographs and the pomegranate is solidly there. It would be interesting to see it in motion.

Maybe the most beautiful pomegranate accompanies Doretta Davanzo Poli's essay on textiles and clothes, in the book she edited with Anne-Marie Deschodt. It is on the upper part of a Fortuny pleated dress in a colour somewhere between dark pink and pale red – Davanzo Poli calls it 'ruby', but what I see in the photograph is a shining rose crossed with rust – and no one reading what I have written will imagine the

colour very well, or at all. It is easy to believe that no two Fortuny dresses were the same colour. The pomegranate is in soft gold, and the image covers the whole chest, above a wide, waist-holding belt with gold decorations on a slightly orange ground. At the centre of the image is a substantial floating pomegranate. It took me some time to see that the image is in fact printed on a transparent overdress in a more mulberry gauze. It took me longer to see what a proliferation of pomegranates surrounded the central one. There are ten regular pomegranate shapes arrayed around the central one, as if growing out of it. Then there is an outer circle, growing right and left out of a gold pendant near the wearer's navel. Then it becomes clear that the outer circle too is composed of triads of upward-pointing pomegranates, somehow sprinkled with quite different and much more realistic burst-open fruits, showing dark seeds. It is pure Fortuny – the image is one whole image, and when one starts to analyse or deconstruct it, it presents many agreeable puzzles and pleasures.

In 1877 Morris designed a completely different pomegranate, which was printed onto cotton and tusser silk by Warners of Braintree. It combines several formal motifs, on an unusually pale (white) ground, covered with an allover pattern of curling fronds of leaves, simply outlined in dark blue, with sprouting small eight-petalled red flowers. The motifs themselves are defined and imposing, outlines in dark blue leaf patterns, containing abstract designs of flower forms, or hemispheres. With most of Morris's work one needs to look closely to see everything and relate all the parts to the whole. Here, if one draws back, and looks at the whole design, all the abstract forms suddenly become solid and very much pomegranates, with sprouting leaves on top, or curved round the fruit, ready to be pulled away. The pomegranate with the high sprout is surrounded by ten smaller fruits on stems, while the fat fruit is surrounded by the small red flowers. All of it – the white ground, the perhaps oriental design, the heavy reds and blues on the light background – are unexpected and disturbing. It is related to the printed cotton Snakeshead of 1876 which has a wonderful combination of small leafy designs in various blues on black, including recognisable (small) snakeshead fritillaries such as we used to find in meadows. There are large imposing motifs in reds and golds standing out from this background, like flames or large leaves, balanced on formalised stems.

These designs make me think of something else Morris said in his lecture, 'Some Hints on Pattern Designing'. The following quotation will be long – Morris's written voice is as exciting as his images. He says that ornamental pattern work must possess three qualities: 'beauty, imagination and order'. Of order, he says that:

> *Without it neither the beauty nor the imagination could be made visible; it is the bond of their life and as good as creates them, if they are to be of any use to people in general. Let us see therefore,*

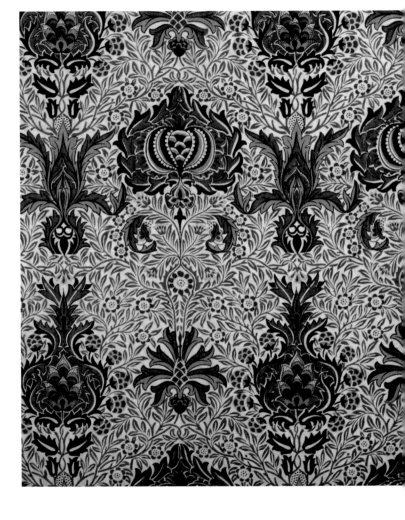

with what instruments it works, how it brings together the material and spiritual sides of the craft.

I have already said something of the way in which it deals with the materials which nature gives it, and how, as it were, it both builds a wall against vagueness and opens a door therein for imagination to come in by. Now this is done by means of treatment which is called, as one may say technically, the conventionalising of nature. That is to say, order invents beautiful and natural forms, which, appealing to a reasonable and imaginative person, will remind him not only of the part of nature which, to his mind at least, they represent, but also of much that lies beyond that part. I have already hinted at some reasons for this treatment of natural objects. You can't bring a whole countryside, or a whole field, into your room, nor even a whole bush; and, moreover, only a very skilled craftsman can make any approach to what might pass with us in moments of excitement for an imitation of such-like things. These are the limitations which are common to every form of the lesser arts; but besides these, every material in which household goods are fashioned imposes certain limitations within which the craftsman must work. Here again, is a wall of order against vagueness, and a door for the imagination. For you must understand from the first that these limitations are as far as possible from being hindrances to beauty in the several crafts. On the contrary, they are incitements and helps to its attainment; those who find them *irksome are not born craftsmen, and the periods of art that try to get rid of them are declining periods.*

The earlier pomegranates by Morris which I have described learn how to show the pomegranate through the patterns of its depiction. They increase both in accuracy and subtlety. This almost abstract order, imposed by its designer as a needlework designer might impose repetitions and variations, is different – it still relies on the order of the shape of growing pomegranates for its own intrinsic order, but the artist has used that order to make a form for quite different shapes of patterns and colours. Altogether they show the endlessness of what is there to be imagined and shaped.

BIRD

In 1916 Proust wrote to his friend Maria Hahn, who was also a close friend of Fortuny, with a string of precise questions about Fortuny's sources and images.

> *Savez-vous du moins si jamais Fortuny dans des robes de chambre*
> *a pris pour motifs de ces oiseaux accouplés, buvant par exemple*
> *dans un vase, qui sont si fréquents à St Marc, dans les chapiteaux*
> *byzantins. Et savez-vous aussi s'il y a à Venise des tableaux (je*
> *voudrais quelques titres) où il y a des manteaux, des robes, dont*
> *Fortuny se serait (ou aurait pu) s'inspirer?*

> *Do you know, at least, whether Fortuny has ever used as a decoration*
> *for his dressing-gowns those pairs of birds, drinking from a vase for*
> *example, which appear so frequently in St Mark's on Byzantine*
> *capitals? And do you know if in Venice there are any paintings (I*
> *would like some titles) in which any coats or dresses appear that*
> *Fortuny may have (or could have) gained inspiration from?*

Maria encouraged him, and Proust in his novel subsequently described Albertine's Fortuny dress, which the narrator had given her.

> *Elle était envahie d'ornementation arabe comme Venise, comme*
> *les palais de Venise dissimulés à la façon des sultanes derrière un*
> *voile ajouré de pierres comme les reliures de la Bibliothèque*

Ambrosienne, comme les colonnes desquelles les oiseaux orientaux
qui signifient alternativement la mort et la vie, se répétaient dans
le miroitement de l'étoffe.

It swarmed with Arabic ornaments like Venice, like the Venetian
palaces hidden like the sultan's wives behind a screen of pierced
stone, like the bindings in the Ambrosian Library, like the columns
from which the oriental birds that symbolised alternately life and
death were repeated in the mirror of the fabric.

Peter Collier has written an amazingly interesting book, *Proust and Venice*, in which he studies Proust's idea of Venice, and the images from Venice which partly inform and construct *À la recherche du temps perdu*. He has two chapters on Fortuny. In the first of these he goes into the birds of Venice. He finds them – particularly phoenixes and peacocks – in the buildings and works of art. And he sees Fortuny as instrumental in the resurrection of the art of the past.

Birds in Venice are like pomegranates – they are recognisably symbolic, and many of them derive from Byzantium and the East, from North African and Arab cultures. As Proust noted, they come in pairs. Sometimes they are face-to-face, sometimes they look away from each other, sometimes their necks are entwined, sometimes they are one two-headed bird. Peter Collier observes that the phoenix is 'a well-known Christian and Venetian symbol but it is not actually prevalent in the city. The peacock is.' He gives a spirited description of symbolic animals and birds in cathedrals, especially in San Marco.

> *It is everywhere the peacock ... symbol of immortality and resurrection, which triumphs in Venice. On either side of the chancel screen in Torcello cathedral a pair of bas-relief peacocks supping from a chalice guards the approach to the altar, and St Mark's (despite being a veritable menagerie of gryphons, St John's eagles, Mark's lions and doves of the holy spirit) reserves pride of place to two enormous pairs of mosaic peacocks, a pair on either side of the floor of the nave, as well as displaying one bas-relief pair on the parapet of the first-floor gallery and another couple of pairs inset in the outer north-west wall. Outside the north front of the basilica is a peacock surmounting a globe, symbolising the triumph of the spirit over the world of earthly desires, and there is another pair of these carved beside the altar steps.*

Ruskin was amazed by the birds. He describes them in *The Stones of Venice*, amongst other beasts.

> *Under foot and over head, a continual succession of crowded imagery, one picture passing into another, as in a dream; forms beautiful and terrible mixed together; dragons and serpents and ravening beasts of prey, and graceful birds that in the midst of them*

drink from running fountains and feed from vases of crystal; the
passions and pleasures of human life symbolised together and the
mystery of its redemption.

This is quoted from Morris's edition of *The Stones of Venice* – a point of contact between Morris and Venice and, at a distance, Fortuny. Ruskin illustrated his text with drawings of the birds inset in the outer wall above the west door. Collier describes this work:

a brace of drinking peacocks above a pair of similar but intertwined
birds, and [Ruskin] copies in the same illustration carvings of
another pair of peacocks drinking from a chalice they perch on, and
also a pair of birds linked at the waist which are either a double
eagle or twin phoenixes (it is difficult to see whether they are on fire
or merely have spiky feathers).

Fortuny's garments are intimately involved in the relationship between the narrator of *À la recherche* and his mistress Albertine, who eventually leaves him, wearing a Fortuny cloak and taking nothing else. A quarrel between the lovers takes place whilst Albertine is wearing a Fortuny dress, which Collier describes as symbolising an 'intricate conjugation of death and desire, art and resurrection'. There has been some discussion as to whether Fortuny made dresses with the phoenixes, eagles and peacocks which are used as symbols elsewhere in the novel. Even if there is no record of a Fortuny dress with images of phoenixes Proust may well have invented one. There is a scene in which the narrator is trying to make love to Albertine, who is wearing a Fortuny dress embellished with birds – phoenixes or peacocks precisely. The narrator tries to make Albertine take off the dress.

> *Since you're being kind enough to stay here a moment to console*
> *me, you ought to take off your gown, it's too hot, too stiff, I dare not*
> *approach you for fear of crumpling that fine stuff, and there are*
> *those fateful birds between us. Undress, my darling.*

The phoenixes or peacocks, *oiseaux fatidiques*, symbolise death and resurrection. The embrace crushes the separate birds together into an embrace of their own, which Albertine experiences as baleful. Marcel kisses her again, and Venice with her.

> *I kissed her then a second time, pressing to my heart the*
> *shimmering golden azure of the Grand Canal and the mating birds,*
> *symbols of death and resurrection. But for the second time, instead*
> *of returning my kiss, she drew away with the sort of instinctive and*
> *baleful obstinacy of animals that feel the hand of death.*

Collier argues: 'It would be in the spirit of Proust's creativity to suppose that the phoenix/peacock motifs are separate on the material, and that we are invited to imagine the embrace itself crushing together in the folds of the cloth birds which are separately drawn.'

The movement of birds on the cloth of dresses and curtains is exciting in itself. Morris too made plans for this. But before leaving the

work of Peter Collier I'd like to mention his elegant and convincing contribution to the discussion of the importance of Fortuny's work, and whether he is original or derivative. Fortuny, he says, was part of the constant movement of death and resurrection of art, which the

birds also signify. Fortuny finds ancient images of creatures, or clothing such as Carpaccio's dresses and jackets, and restores them to new life. Proust presents this in terms of the drinking birds.

> These Fortuny gowns, one of which I had seen Madame de
> Guermantes wearing, were those which Elstir, when he told us about
> the magnificent garments of the women of Carpaccio's and Titian's
> day, had promised would imminently return from their ashes, as
> magnificent as of old, for everything must return in time, as it is
> written beneath the vaults of St Mark's, and proclaimed, as they
> drink from the urns of marble and jasper of the Byzantine capitals,
> by the birds which symbolise at once death and resurrection.

Fortuny the artist, Proust affirms, is the agent of resurrection – as Collier says, Proust 'sets his derivative dress-designer, Fortuny, at the apex of creativity'.

And Collier illustrates this with two pieces of cloth from the Museo Fortuny – one 'designed after a twelfth-century Byzantine original' depicting 'a series of two-headed eagles' with 'strikingly peacock-like plumage', and one with two dancing fighting birds, facing each other, wings outstretched.

De Osma also reproduces images of Fortuny fabrics where naturalistic birds appear as part of the general impression of a design. There is a cotton with a sixteenth-century Italian-style motif which shows a trellis with climbing vines in a mixture of dull reds and greens, with leaves and bunches of fruits. It takes a moment to see that there is a bird there at all. It is hidden behind stems and leaves and is the same colour as they are. Its sharp-beaked naturalistic head can be seen pecking at the stem. Its tail merges into the foliage and the shadows. It is hard to see, and would be even more difficult if the cloth were moving. On a cotton fabric with images inspired by Persian textiles is a row of tiny birds melding into the background, again almost invisible because they are so small. I have wondered who was meant to make these images out and how. What is the beholder meant to see on a sweeping gown or a folded coat? I had never asked myself that. I will come back to it.

Stephen Coote, in his book *William Morris: His Life and Work*, juxtaposes Morris's wonderful Peacock and Dragon (1878) with a fourteenth-century Sicilian textile in the Victoria and Albert Museum. Peacock and Dragon is one of Morris's best-loved and most complex textiles. The Sicilian textile has a repeated image of a pair of birds back-to-back and turning their heads – with hawk or eagle beaks – to glare balefully at each other. The juxtaposition makes it evident just how much Morris had learned from his studies in the V&A. But Peacock and Dragon is very different from most of Morris's woven or painted birds. I am very attached to his first attempt to depict birds, which he did on his first known embroidery in 1857. This is a woollen hanging, If I Can (Morris's personal motto), which has a simple

pattern of alternating trees bearing red and yellow fruits, and some hunched creatures which I think of as the Flat Bird. The art historian Linda Parry refers to this creature as 'over-stylised', but I would call it uncouth. It has two flattish slabs, tapering towards the left end, on top of each other, with a beak shape at the top right. I am not sure, looking at it in reproduction, whether it has an eye – there is no attempt at feet. Apparently it was once brightly coloured in aniline dyed crewel wools, which have now faded to ghostly browns. After this, the birds on Morris's tapestries and other images were worked by others, including Philip Webb and May Morris who was very skilled with birds. Birds in Morris's earlier works seem to sit or stand upon the foliage, having been added later. But already in 1877 Morris was writing to Thomas Wardle, saying he was studying birds in order to put them into his next design. Linda Parry reproduces the original watercolour design for Rose, a printed textile on which small, vaguely thrush-like birds are placed among the rose branches, two clinging to them, another two pairs standing on the ground between the leaves. These birds, like many of Morris's birds, are peaceable and plump, a kind of generic garden bird. After staring at many birds in many books, I have come to the tentative conclusion that they look like living creatures if they have a pupil in their eye, and like part of the overall design if they do not. They are amiable, static birds.

One of Morris's most-loved designs is Bird, a woollen double cloth which he made for his own drawing room at Kelmscott House in

Hammersmith. There are alternating horizontal rows of pairs of birds. There are mild, alert pairs of standing birds, looking over their shoulders towards each other, above pairs of open-winged birds hovering and surveying the pomegranate in the leafy design that contains them. Their precisely observed twiggy legs and clawed feet, their precisely observed tail feathers and wing feathers are pleasing in their generic reminiscence of birds in general. They are designs as Morris wrote of designs – generalisations that also show something of the particular presence of the birds. The background – a bluish green on indigo, thick with leaves and flowers touched in red and gold – is full of arrested life. There are tulips and roses, daisies and something resembling a daffodil, sunflowers and curling tendrils, all in the same three colours, which make the red head, legs and tail of the standing bird stand out, rhythmically. Linda Parry also shows a photograph of this hanging in place in the drawing room at Kelmscott House. It is both peaceful and interesting. Parry quotes a visitor on

> *... a most harmonious and peaceful house ... most exquisitely kept. In dirty Hammersmith, it was as clean as the cleanest country house and the beautiful blue tapestry hanging all round the big living room, with its four windows on the river, looked as if they had just been hung up ... the atmosphere was deliciously homely.*

Strawberry Thief, a printed cotton design, was made much later, in 1883, when Morris had moved to Merton Abbey and, after much effort and many problems, had mastered the difficult technique of indigo discharge. Strawberry Thief was the first indigo-discharge textile to include yellow and red on the lovely blue ground. It has a repeat of four birds, two perched on stylised green fronds, clearly singing lustily, and two beneath them or above them, amongst luscious strawberry plants with clear red berries, each bird carrying away a fruit held by the stalk. Morris said he had observed the birds in his own garden, making their way in under the protective netting and stealing the strawberries. He gave strict instructions that the birds were not to be chased away or disturbed. These birds have delicious sharp claws, strong beaks and lively eyes. They are the same colours – freckled breasts, grey or brown wings and tails – as the earlier ones. They are not thrushes, though they remind us of them. The colours of the textile are clear, strong, unexpected and splendid. There is a wonderful clear pale blue on the dark blue, mixed into an olivey leaf green, and there are patterns, both intricate and clear, of flowers, and flower buds, leaves and curling tendrils. Everything is balanced and orderly; everything is running riot; everything is an English garden.

CODA

This writing began, as I said, with an involuntary visual experience – Kelmscott behind closed eyes, with the meandering Thames and grass fields, when I was in the dark mysterious space of the Palazzo Fortuny. Later, I closed my eyes in Walthamstow, in the William Morris Gallery, and saw the stones and canals of Venice. I wanted to write about Fortuny, whose work I didn't then know at all, but Morris wouldn't go away. So I embarked on an essay without knowing what I should find.

Morris, as I said, I knew. I have studied his writing, and looked at his fabrics and wallpapers. We have Morris in our house. I eat my breakfast sitting on a faded Morris cushion with woodpecker and apple branches. We have a window with heavy Morris curtains ... Our living room is papered with Willow Boughs and our tea towels have Morris flowers in rose and green complications. I eat my lunch from a teatray also covered in Willow Boughs. Our kitchen is tiled with Seaweed, which turned out in fact to be designed by John Henry Dearle, and has something which always excites me in Morris designs – a deeper allover background under the pale blue flowers and coiling seaweed leaves in different greens. I am drawn to Morris patterns which have an under-pattern of tiny dark leaves of evergreens. I don't think we chose these designs out of a particular devotion to Morris – they were just the most exciting things we found. Both the colours and the geometry and, as Morris hoped, the reality of real flowers and leaves.

Fortuny was a whole new visual world to learn – fabrics and colours designed for the human body, as well as for elegant spaces. Silks and velvets never the same colour twice – the exhibition I saw in New York had a group of elegant dresses on stands, the subtle dyes always different, enhancing each other. Panache, grace, startling, calm. Someone in whose gallery I went to see Fortuny's fabrics in London gave me a strip of dyed cloth, with a border of the same cloth in a different design. It sits on my desk. It is patterned in a rusty red-brown on two different dusty greens, the fabric, patterned with flowers, just darker and bluer than the border. Through the day, through changes of weather, the colours change, bluer, greener, the brown sandier, more russet at different times. I like looking at colours, just for the sake of looking at colours. It is always surprising how people don't really *look* at things. I was once in a gallery where there was an exhibition of Monet's paintings of Rouen Cathedral. I sat on a bench to look at them, in bright painted sunlight, in shadow, in simple daylight. A steady stream of people walked, without stopping, between me and the paintings, turning their heads briefly to note each one. What did they see, what did they remember? I, on the other hand, tried to make my brain record tiny juxtapositions of greys and browns, notations of shade and brightness. It is not possible to remember whole cathedrals, only impressions. But it is exciting to try.

I have taken so much sensual pleasure in this Fortuny–Morris project. I can't hear music, really, and I think I give colours all the attention I have spare from not listening to sounds. I collected an unmanageable heap of large books on Fortuny and Morris, and had the same light-shadow experience. When I was looking at sleek Fortuny I couldn't imagine the briefly fading and occluded Morris. When I turned to Morris, there was all the life of the vegetable world, the colours of growing things, the geometry of branches and petals and fruits. And Fortuny faded temporarily to a transparent shadow.

When I began this essay I didn't know how much it was going to be about another thing that obsesses me as a reader and a writer. Work. E.M. Forster once remarked sagaciously that novelists do not give work the importance it has in real life, not as much as love and death. And here I had not one but two obsessive workers, endlessly inventive, endlessly rigorous, endlessly beautiful. They both made the place where they lived identical with the place where they worked. They were both hands-on, with the dyeing and pleating, with the block-printing, with research about how to do things differently or better. They both invented new colours and resurrected old and discarded ones, using vegetable dyes not aniline ones (on the whole). They researched their subject with passion, and had large libraries, specialist and general. I was pleased to note that the first book about dyes that Morris bought was the first book written specifically on the art of dyeing, and was a Venetian book written in 1540. It was by Giovanni Ventura Roseto, *Plictho de l'arte de tentori*, which Morris said was hard to translate, which means he did translate it.

Finally, two works of art, one by each artist. First Mariano Fortuny y Madrazo, a dress from the Museo del Traje, Madrid. It is called Eleonora (1920–30), and is made of silk velvet, silk satin, silk cording and glass beads. It is black, long-sleeved, with an inserted group of pleats in a mixture of brownish gold and fading grey in the side, fastened with russet cord, and the lovely Venetian Murano beads which Fortuny chose himself from the glass-blowers. These are black and white and oval. There are beads also along the underside of the long sleeves. I don't know if it was made for Eleonora Duse – there seem to be many dresses with her name in essays about Fortuny's work. From a distance it rises from hem to neck, gleaming with regular silver curves of mounting fruits and stems. Only when you look more closely can you see the other ingredients of the pattern, which is dense and complex though it looks so orderly. Then you see that there is a mounting pattern of starbursts crowned with what appear to be fronds, within the curves of the fruit branches. Then you notice the tiny living creatures – a heraldic lion prancing, looking backwards and holding a screed which coils into the rays of the sun. And tiny open-winged birds, lively and also prancing, and also looking backwards in front of the curving fruit-branches. What I love about this design is the combination of the overall order of the repeating curves, moving up the body, and the detail at close quarters. I imagine that most people, seeing a woman in this subtle dress, would not be close enough to read the detail at all. You would need to be standing quite intimately near her. I thought, as

I thought more and more as I saw more of Fortuny, of how his fabrics are made to move and fold with a moving body, to reveal themselves in part, changing as they move. I go back to this dress often, and study it, as I also go back to my final image from William Morris, Peacock and Dragon.

There is a fourteenth-century Sicilian textile in the V&A which has the double birds, almost joined at the tails, turned away from each other and looking fiercely backwards. These alternate with horizontal rows of lively hunting dogs. Morris's Peacock and Dragon is sumptuous in green and gold. Horizontal lines of golden dragons alternate with horizontal lines of more shadowy peacocks in a redder gold and a shadowy green. They have wonderful curved necks, echoing each other, mouths open to hiss or shoot flame, static and aggressive. The peacocks have proud feet and tails; the dragons curve downwards out of a formal flame. The green background is formal too, and full of green flowers and leaves that make one surface. These are designed to occupy a proud space – a large wall. The whole surface is splendidly integrated and full of interesting detail. Like the Fortuny dress, Peacock and Dragon is brilliant, complicated and simple. I look at them again and again.

FURTHER READING

FORTUNY

FORTUNY E WAGNER, Paolo Bolpagni,
Fondazione Musei Civici di Venezia, 2012

WAGNER AND THE ART OF THE THEATRE, Patrick Carnegy,
Yale University Press, 2006

PROUST AND VENICE, Peter Collier,
Cambridge University Press, 1989

FORTUNY, Anne-Marie Deschodt and Doretta Davanzo Poli,
Harry N. Abrams Inc., 2001

FASHION MEMOIR: Fortuny, Delphine Desveaux,
Thames & Hudson, 1998

THE SECRETS OF THE GRAND CANAL, Alberto Toso Fei,
Studio LT2, 2010

MARIANO FORTUNY: La seta e il velluto, Jean-Pierre Gabriel,
Fondazione Musei Civici di Venezia, 2010

KNOSSOS AND THE PROPHETS OF MODERNISM, Cathy Gere,
University of Chicago Press, 2009

LE MANTEAU DE FORTUNY, Gérard Macé,
Gallimard, 1987

FORTUNY: The Life and Work of Mariano Fortuny, Guillermo de Osma,
Rizzoli, 1980

FORTUNY ET PROUST: Venise, les Ballets Russes, Guillermo de Osma,
L'Echoppe, 2014

THE FORTUNY MUSEUM IN PALAZZO PESARO DEGLI ORFEI, VENICE,
Skira Guides, 2008

FORTUNY Y MADRAZO: An Artistic Legacy, Molly Sorkin and Jennifer Park, eds.
Queen Sofía Spanish Institute, 2012

MORRIS

JOHN RUSKIN, Arts Council Exhibition,
Arts Council of Great Britain, 1983

THE FLOWERS OF WILLIAM MORRIS, Derek Baker,
Barn Elms Publishing, 1996

WILLIAM MORRIS: His Life and Work, Stephen Coote,
Garamond, 1990

WILLIAM MORRIS'S KELMSCOTT: Landscape and History, A. Crossley,
T. Hassall and P. Salway, eds.,
Windgather Press, 2007

SELECTED POEMS OF WILLIAM MORRIS, Peter Faulkner, ed.,
Carcanet, 1992

QUESTIONS OF TRAVEL: William Morris in Iceland, Lavinia Greenlaw,
Notting Hill Editions, 2004

THE GARDENS OF WILLIAM MORRIS, Jill, Duchess of Hamilton, Penny Hart
and John Simmons, Stewart, Tabori and Chang, 1998

WILLIAM MORRIS: A Life for Our Time, Fiona MacCarthy,
Faber & Faber, 1994

THE EARTHLY PARADISE, William Morris,
Longmans & Co., 1903

NEWS FROM NOWHERE AND OTHER WRITINGS, William Morris,
Penguin Classics, 1993

THE STORY OF SIGURD THE VOLSUNG AND THE FALL OF THE NIBLUNGS,
William Morris,
Longmans & Co., 1904

THE WELL AT THE WORLD'S END, William Morris,
Longmans & Co., 1896

RED HOUSE, National Trust,
National Trust Enterprises Ltd., 2003

WILLIAM MORRIS: Artist, Craftsman, Pioneer, R. Ormiston and N. M. Wells,
Flame Tree Publishing, 2010

WILLIAM MORRIS AND THE ART OF EVERYDAY LIFE, Wendy Parkins, ed.,
Cambridge Scholars Publishing, 2010

TEXTILES OF THE ARTS & CRAFTS MOVEMENT, Linda Parry,
Thames & Hudson, 1998

WILLIAM MORRIS: Art and Kelmscott, Linda Parry, ed.,
Boydell, 1996

WILLIAM MORRIS TEXTILES, Linda Parry,
V&A Publishing, 2013

DANTE GABRIEL ROSSETTI, Ernest Radford,
George Newnes Ltd., 1905

THE NATURE OF GOTHIC, John Ruskin,
Euston Grove Press, 2008

THE NATURE OF GOTHIC, John Ruskin,
Kelmscott Press, 1892

WILLIAM MORRIS AND THE ARTS & CRAFTS HOME, Pamela Todd,
Thames & Hudson, 2005

V&A PATTERN: William Morris,
V&A Publishing, 2009

WILLIAM MORRIS AS DESIGNER, Ray Watkinson,
Van Nostrand Reinhold, 1967

ESSENTIAL WILLIAM MORRIS, Iain Zaczek,
Parragon, 2000

FORTUNY & MORRIS

THE STONES OF VENICE, John Ruskin,
Da Capo Press, 1960

LIST OF ILLUSTRATIONS

NORTH & SOUTH

FABRICS, DESIGNS & LIGHT

POMEGRANATE

BIRD

CODA

Photographic credits: Palazzo Pesaro Orfei, 5, 18, 60, 86, 115 © FCMV, Fortuny Museum Archive; 4, 12 ©National Portrait Gallery, London; 8, 10 ©Tate, London 2016; 16 Courtesy of Museo de la Biblioteca Nacional de Espana, Madrid; 26 ©National Trust Images/Andrew Butler; 30, 154 ©Society of Antiquaries, London (Kelmscott Manor); 32, 34, 41, 113, 152, 156, Willow Boughs endpaper (back) ©William Morris Gallery, London Borough of Waltham Forest; 47, 74 ©Country Life; 50, 64, 77, 118, 133, 148 ©Claudio Franzini for Fortuny Museum; 78 Courtesy of Cornell University Library (Icelandic and Faroese Photographs of Frederick W.W. Howell); 90 ©Bridgeman Images; 94 ©Ashmolean Museum, University of Oxford; 127, 136, 158 ©Victoria and Albert Museum, London; 166 ©Museo del Traje, Madrid/Photo Munio Rodil Ares; 170, 182 ©Fabrizio Giraldi; Delphos gown endpaper (front) ©1stdibs.com

ACKNOWLEDGEMENTS

This little book grew out of an invitation to visit Venice, from Shaul Bassi and Flavio Gregori of Ca' Foscari University of Venice, for the Incroci di Civiltà (Crossings of Civilisations) literary festival in May 2011, jointly organised by Ca' Foscari University, the Municipality of Venice and the Fondazione Musei Civici di Venezia. The visit was very happy and I am very grateful for the invitation. I should like to thank Shaul and Flavio for everything they did for my husband and myself. And I should like to thank my Italian publishers, Einaudi – in particular Andrea Canobbio.

I should also like to thank Daniela Ferretti, the Director of the Museo Fortuny and her colleagues Cristina Da Roit and Dennis Cecchin.

We were made very welcome at Morris's houses, the Red House at Bexleyheath, Kelmscott Manor in Gloucestershire, and the William Morris Gallery in Walthamstow. The William Morris Gallery recently won a prize for Museum of the Year and is splendidly and inventively designed. Rowan Bain, Anna Mason and Gary Heales have been extremely helpful with the illustrations and design of this book. We discovered Peta Smyth Antique Textiles, in Pimlico, where we were shown many Fortuny fabrics, and told about dyes and designs.

As ever my publishers Chatto & Windus have been both efficient and imaginative. I should like particularly to thank my editor, Jenny Uglow, my publisher, Clara Farmer, and Charlotte Humphery. Very few authors can have been given such care and enthusiasm with the choice of illustrations. I am also grateful to my editor at Alfred A. Knopf, Robin Desser.

Stephen Parker has designed this book with his usual brilliance and care, both inside and out.

My Italian translators and friends, Anna Nadotti and Fausto Galuzzi have been both helpful and enthusiastic, as always.

My agent, Zoe Waldie, at Rogers Coleridge and White, has been steadily supportive and full of ideas, as have my agents at ILA, Sam Edenborough and Nicki Kennedy. In America, thanks to my agent, Melanie Jackson, and my lecture agent, Steven Barclay, who shared some of his knowledge about Fortuny's world.

I could not have written this book without Fiona MacCarthy, whose scholarship and wit bring Morris and his world to life. She has become a friend during my work on this book and has answered all sorts of questions.

Thanks to my husband, Peter Duffy, for much more than patience with the usual habits of writers. We have visited galleries together, both in Venice and in England, and his ideas are always exciting and useful.

And I am lucky that my assistant, Gill Marsden, came back – as I was reaching the end of this book – after ten years in Wales and made my life almost orderly. It is true that I can never thank her enough.

A NOTE ON THE TYPE

This book is set in Golden Cockerel, a font Eric Gill drew for The Golden Cockerel Press.

William Morris set a precedent for private presses using their own proprietary font when he designed Golden for the Kelmscott Press. This roman typeface, derived largely from that created by Nicolas Jenson in Venice in 1476, was used for the press's first publication, *The Story of the Glittering Plain*, in 1891.

The Golden Cockerel Press was founded in 1920. When Robert Gibbings took control in 1924 he wanted to create a type which was true to the Arts and Crafts spirit of the private press. Eric Gill designed Golden Cockerel in 1929 and it was first used in A.E. Coppard's *The Hundredth Story* in 1931.